JAMES BOND

THE SECRET WORLD OF

007™

Written by
Alastair Dougall

Illustrated by
Roger Stewart

Consultant Editor
Dave Worrall

A Dorling Kindersley Book

CONTENTS

JAMES BOND

THE SECRET WORLD OF

LONDON, NEW YORK, MUNICH, MELBOURNE, AND DELHI

Senior Editor Alastair Dougall
Senior Art Editors Gary Hyde, Jill Bunyan
Designer Dan Bunyan
Brand Manager Lisa Lanzarini
Managing Art Editor Jacquie Gulliver
Publishing Managers Karen Dolan, Simon Beecroft
Category Publisher Alex Allan
Picture Research Kate Duncan, Martin Copeland, Sarah Stewart-Richardson
Production Controllers Chris Avgherinos, Rochelle Talary, Amy Bennett
Production Editor Clare McLean
DTP Designers Jill Bunyan, Sue Wright, Hanna Ländin

First published in Great Britain in 2000 by Dorling Kindersley Limited.
This paperback edition published in Great Britain in 2011 by Dorling Kindersley Limited,
80 Strand, London WC2R 0RL

A Penguin Company

11 12 13 14 10 9 8 7 6 5 4 3 2 1

A CIP catalogue record for this book is available from the British Library.

ISBN: 978-1-4053-7086-8

Colour reproduction by Colourscan, Singapore
Printed and bound in China by Hung Hing Offset Printing

THE MOVIES 156

FOREWORD

Just a few years ago a book like this would have been unthinkable. The suggestion that MI6 case files should be opened in order to celebrate the career of a single Double-O agent – James Bond – would have met with amused incredulity (or apoplectic rage!) in government circles.

Happily, times and attitudes change: part of my brief when I became head of Her Majesty's Secret Service was to illuminate some of MI6's darker corners. So, in accordance with this spirit of greater openness, I am delighted to present *James Bond: the Secret World of 007.*

Many readers will already be familiar with the name Bond (it has proved impossible to keep his exploits entirely "under wraps"); however, all of us at MI6 are confident that these pages will shed fresh light on the missions – and unique personality – of Agent Double-O-Seven and, perhaps most exciting of all, the extraordinary vehicles and gadgetry supplied by Q Branch for his use "in the field".

M

THE BOND DOSSIER

Even to those closest to him at MI6, the counter-intelligence wing of the British Secret Service, Bond remains an enigma. A loner, with his own fierce code of honour, he seems to have been born to be a spy. An unerring ability to think on his feet, superb fighting skills and an unwavering commitment to any mission, however dangerous, have made him the first agent that his boss, M, turns to in times of crisis. Of course, MI6 does not send their best man out "into the field" without back-up – Q Branch's hi-tech wizardry ensures that 007 always has a trick up his elegant sleeve.

Countless women have fallen for Bond, irresistibly drawn to his self-confidence, his sense of style, his sardonic humour, and the aura of danger that surrounds him. Yet none is allowed to get too close. For the world of international espionage James Bond inhabits is one in which death may strike at any moment, where no one is truly innocent, where everyone has a secret agenda.

LICENSED TO KILL

Three gold-braid bands denote the rank of Commander.

MI6 coat of arms

AFTER RISING TO THE rank of Commander in the British navy, Bond joined MI6, becoming one of the few agents "licensed to kill". His role is to track down those who seek world domination and the destruction of Western civilization. Nothing stops him in this battle with ultimate evil.

MILITARY MAN
Bond remains proud of his naval career. He donned his Commander's uniform as part of his cover when visiting an American military base during the *Tomorrow Never Dies* assignment.

"FOR YOUR EYES ONLY"

TO: THE PRIME MINSTER

SUBJECT: JAMES BOND, 007

In reply to your enquiry voicing natural concern about the potential international repercussions of the above agent's actions, you have my personal assurance that, had it not been for 007's intervention, disaster on a global scale would certainly have resulted. The Service will, of course, dispose of the inevitable débris and handle any media fall-out.

All good wishes

M

DEADLY AIM
A knife is easier to conceal and quieter than any gun; Bond often employs a Fairbairn-Sykes. He has undergone full commando training and is extremely good at hand-to-hand combat with this weapon. He is also an expert knife-thrower.

The Fairbairn-Sykes knife was standard British commando issue in World War II.

JAMES BOND 007

- **Height:** 6 ft 1 in (183 cm)
- **Weight:** 12 stone (76 kg)
- **Distinguishing marks:** Scar on right shoulder; back of right hand
- **Education:** Eton and Fettes; Cambridge University (First in Oriental languages)
- **Other Languages:** French, German (fluent); also Italian, Greek, Czech, Russian

A Walther P99 gave Bond extra firepower on his Tomorrow Never Dies *mission*

Bond is the most accurate shot in the Service.

Shoulder holster

Walther PPK

Disguised as a manta ray, 007 fooled enemy surveillance during his Licence to Kill mission

Bond risked life and limb to reach the villain's clifftop lair on the For Your Eyes Only assignment

CRACK SHOT

Bond's remarkable accuracy with any kind of firearm is not just natural talent, but the product of long hours on the MI6 shooting range.

BY STEALTH

Bond has no equal at infiltrating the defences of an enemy. The success of his missions – and his own survival – frequently relies on his expertise as a frogman (left) or a mountaineer

7.65 mm ammo is easy to obtain around the world

Weight: 580 g

Magazine release

Bond never gives up during a fight, however desperate the situation

Length: 148 mm

FAVOURITE GUN

Worn in a shoulder holster under his left arm, the lightweight Walther PPK is Bond's favoured handgun. It first appeared in 1931 and was especially designed for the German plain-clothes police. It is reliable, easy to conceal, and draw, thanks to its streamlined shape. At night, Bond sleeps with it under his pillow.

Magazine floorplate may be flat (as here) or with polymer finger rest

Short butt

THE KILLING GAME

Bond kills out of self-defence and takes little pleasure in the deed. At times – particularly if the victim is a beautiful woman – he has even felt a pang of regret. He represses his feelings with sardonic humour. He knows that remorse would jeopardise the success of his mission, dull his reflexes, and probably cost him his life.

6-round magazine

SHOULDER THROW

The advantage of this move is that it turns an opponent's superior weight into a disadvantage – the bigger they are, the harder they fall!

Opponent

1. Step across with right foot, turn your back on opponent. Release your right hand.

2. Drop under his centre of gravity. Push right biceps muscle against underside of his right arm. Grasp his sleeve with right hand.

3. Bend sharply forwards and lever opponent over your back.

MARTIAL ARTS TRAINING

Bond is not an expert at any particular martial arts discipline; however he does have a grounding in the basics of judo, ju-jitsu, and karate. When faced by opponents larger than himself, judo has proved extremely useful.

THE BOND "LOOK"

Brioni was Bond's favourite tailor

THE WAY JAMES BOND presents himself to the world – his "look" – provides a number of telling insights into his personality. As befits his public persona of a successful businessman for Universal Exports, his style is undemonstrative and classically tailored, suggesting a man at ease with himself and in control of his life. He favours lightweight suits in muted shades for most occasions, and a tuxedo for formal events. Shoes, shirts, and ties are of the best quality. Everything fits, nothing is left to chance – he transcends the whims of fashion.

STRONG SUIT
Bond's suits are tailored with great care to withstand wear and tear.

TIES
Bond's ties do not distract from the face. They are hand-made from woven silk.

Black Oxfords

Heel pulls back on springs

SUMMER WEIGHT
In hot climates, Bond both stays and looks cool in a crisp, white cotton shirt and a lightweight, linen-and-cotton-mix suit. Whether off-duty or on assignment, a fast car and a beautiful companion are rarely far away.

HOMING DEVICE
Without jeopardizing comfort, Q Branch adapted one of Bond's shoes to carry a homing device. This fitted into a compartment beneath the heel. The homer allowed the CIA's Felix Leiter to keep track of 007 during the *Goldfinger* mission.

SHOES
Bond's footwear is of classic design, hard-wearing, and hand-made in black or brown leather. His shoes are always polished – a reminder of his military background.

Homing device

BATTLE DRESS
When Bond has the opportunity to prepare for a showdown with the enemy he may wear black army fatigues.

Cotton voile dress shirt

Bond never wears a clip-on tie

A linen handkerchief completes the outfit

Pearl studs

HARD MAN
When infiltrating a terrorist arms market during the *Tomorrow Never Dies* assignment, Bond wore a heavy-duty leather jacket, giving him the air of a tough resistance fighter.

DISCREET LINKS
Cuff links complete the formal look. Bond's are small and undemonstrative.

FOR DISGUISE ONLY
On assignment, Bond occasionally wears glasses, to project a business-like image. The lenses are plain glass, of course – he has 20/20 vision.

BELTS
For the *GoldenEye* mission, Q provided Bond with a rappelling device in his belt. An explosive charge powered a piton and a 22.5-metre-long (75 ft) cord.

Clasp swings open

Firing button for explosive device

Coiled steel-reinforced cord easily bore Bond's weight

Opening firing-plate arms piton and accesses firing button

EVENING DRESS
In many ways, a tuxedo is Bond's quintessential uniform. The jacket is single-breasted, black or white with narrow lapels; the dress shirt soft-fronted with pearl studs.

Barbed piton ensured secure grip on concrete or brick

Spanish leather

Watch doubles as a gadget

Dress trousers are narrow-cut, lending a military flavour

BOND IN LOVE

FOR JAMES BOND, a beautiful woman, especially an independent, free-spirited woman, is an irresistible challenge – the ultimate prize of a life lived as if there were no tomorrow. Love never lasts long in Bond's world. As Paris Carver, a former lover, once remarked, with tragic foresight: "This job of yours – it's murder on relationships." So Bond keeps moving, from romance to romance. Yet one name will always linger in his memory – the name of his murdered bride, Tracy di Vicenzo.

SYLVIA
Bond met Sylvia Trench at a London casino just before he left on the *Dr. No* assignment. He enjoyed her sense of fun, but she grew impatient with his "here today, gone tomorrow" lifestyle.

EXTRA FIZZ
Having an old-fashioned streak, Bond has always found that ice-cold champagne adds sparkle to romance.

TRACY
The only time Bond ever dreamed of settling down was when he fell in love with Teresa ("Tracy") di Vicenzo. Their bliss was shattered by a burst of machine-gun fire. She is the one woman Bond has never, ever forgotten.

PARIS
Bond broke off their love-affair when she "got too close for comfort". He still had powerful feelings for her when they met again, years later. By then she was the wife of press baron Elliot Carver.

FATAL ATTRACTIONS

Dangerous women are Bond's fatal weakness. With no commitment – with no quarter – offered on either side, he plunges into affairs with fatal femmes – often just for the sheer hell of it.

MAY DAY
She liked to be in control – and she was!

ENIA ONATOPP
Bond and Xenia shared a love of fast cars and double entendres, but her love-making style was just too violent – even for 007.

HELGA BRANDT
This tigerish SPECTRE agent tried to have her cake and eat it – but was eaten herself ...

FALLEN ANGELS
In contrast to his cynical side, Bond has a strong, chivalrous urge to rescue and protect women who have unjustly suffered at the hands of fate and other men. Sometimes, Bond has found it very hard to say goodbye.

ELEKTRA KING

Few women have posed a greater threat to Bond's equilibrium than Elektra. Her bewitching charm made his heart believe she was a persecuted victim; but his head told him she was a murderous psychopath.

DOMINO
She risked her life to avenge her brother and save thousands of lives – Bond could not let her down.

NATALYA
An innocent witness of mass murder pursued by killers – how could Bond resist her?

FRIENDLY AGENTS
Experiencing life-or-death situations in exotic locales creates all kinds of tensions in a superspy. Add a beautiful, intelligent foreign agent, such as Anya Amasova (left) for a perfect recipe for romance 007-style.

THE "SERVICE"

MI6 crest

WORKING TIRELESSLY around the clock whenever national security is threatened, the staff of MI6, Her Majesty's Secret Service, are the closest Bond has – and will probably ever have – to a family. The backroom mainstays of this close-knit unit are M, the chief, Miss Moneypenny, M's secretary, and chief of staff Bill Tanner. In recent times, the service's all-male ethos was broken when a woman became the new M (all MI6 heads are nicknamed M). At first, Bond and Tanner thought little of her. However, she soon made them think again.

M

Taking up her position as the new head of MI6 shortly before the *GoldenEye* case, the sheer force of M's personality quickly impressed Bond. He and his close friend Bill Tanner had assumed she was little better than a time-serving accountant, "a bean-counter". She quickly put Bond in his place, calling him "a sexist, misogynist dinosaur," and adding that she had no compunction about sending a man to his death but that she would not do it "on a whim".

MISS MONEYPENNY
M's personal assistant is utterly dedicated to her work, which means she has little time for a social life. A close confidante of her boss, she also enjoys a flirtatious, mocking relationship with 007, whom she understands perfectly.

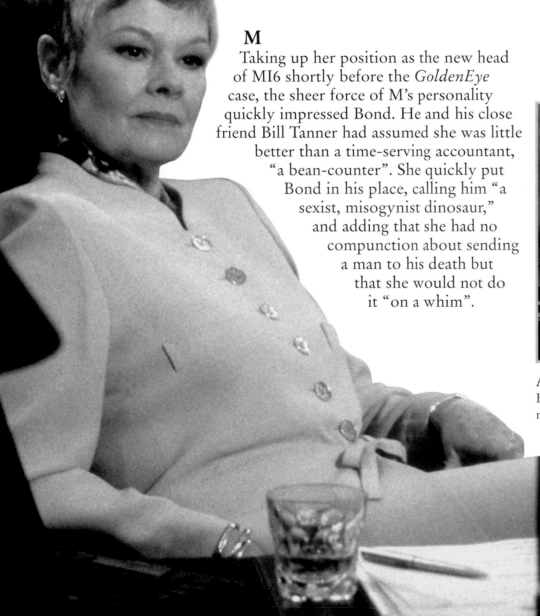

ALONE ON THE BRIDGE
Facing down furious opposition from male colleagues, making rapid decisions when the stakes seem impossibly high, M has learned that the MI6 Operations Room can be a very lonely place indeed.

HOMES AND HIDEOUTS

Following the explosion at MI6, the office moved to a remote castle in Scotland (left). When the Service needs a base "in the field", unexpected places are chosen, such as the wreck of the *Queen Elizabeth* in Hong Kong harbour for Bond's *The Man With the Golden Gun* mission.

BOMB BLAST

The only time MI6's internal security has been breached was at the start of *The World Is Not Enough* case, when a bomb in one of the offices ripped a hole in an exterior wall.

CHANGING BASES

MI6's HQ is on the Thames Embankment in London. However, when necessary, the Service has "set up shop" in a number of secret locations – the better to monitor the activities of a certain double-O agent.

Dr Warmflash noted Bond's "exceptional stamina"

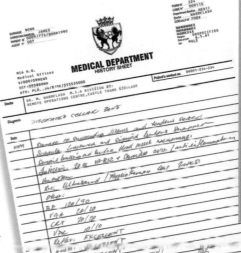

ROBINSON

Calm and reliable, Robinson proved a very able deputy for Bill Tanner while the latter was on leave during the *Tomorrow Never Dies* case. He is now one of the most trusted members of M's staff.

DOCTOR WARMFLASH

Bond generally avoids office romances, but in the case of Dr Molly Warmflash he made an exception. In return, she gave him clean bill of health.

UNDER PRESSURE

M faced her toughest test with *The World Is Not Enough* crisis. Not only was MI6's London HQ directly attacked, she was a personal friend of one of the main victims, Sir Robert King, and of his daughter Elektra.

BILL TANNER

Superb in a crisis, and blessed with a dry sense of humour, Tanner is M's Chief of Staff. He is also Bond's staunchest ally in the Service, and they often enjoy a round of golf when off-duty. A family man, Tanner is just a little envious of Bond's freedom.

THE WIZARD OF MI6

FOR YEARS the brilliant, eccentric, yet immensely likeable Major Boothroyd, known simply as "Q", worked his magic behind the scenes at MI6. Whenever escape seemed impossible, agent after agent – even 007, though he would probably never admit it – owed their lives to this wizard of technology. Q never expected gratitude; all he hoped was that his meticulously crafted machines would be returned "in pristine order". This survey of some of his less well-known inventions, displays just a fraction of the breadth and originality of his work for Q Branch.

A LOT OF HOT AIR
Q stopped by in this patriotic balloon to pick up 007 at the end of the *Octopussy* mission.

ON LOCATION
On several of 007's missions, Q set up workshops to be close to the action. For the *The Spy Who Loved Me* assignment, his base was hidden deep inside an Egyptian pyramid.

A FRIEND INDEED
"Thought I'd pop round" – Q risked M's wrath by helping out 007 when the latter went AWOL in central America during the *Licence to Kill* mission. Here he shows Bond's friend, Pam Bouvier, a polaroid camera that fires a laser beam.

Q AND 007
Q took his work seriously and was often irritated by Bond's frivolous quips. "Now pay attention, Double-O-Seven," he would sigh as, like a weary schoolmaster, he began to brief Bond on his latest invention. Bond rarely seemed to be listening, but Q knew that he had an intuitive grasp of how to get the very best from any new equipment. Q's only real complaint was that hardly a single item ever came back intact.

WATCH THIS!
One of Q's great skills was his ability to incorporate exotic features – a laser beam, a rapelling line, a buzzsaw – into 007's various "standard issue" watches.

Face lights up like a torch

LIFELINE
Bond used Q's rapelling watch to escape death during *The World Is Not Enough* mission.

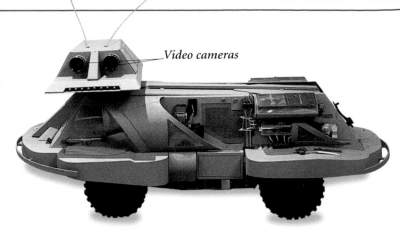

Video cameras

"SNOOPER"
"A new pet, Q?" Bond inquired, raising an eyebrow. Q tested this "highly sophisticated surveillance machine" at the end of the *A View to a Kill* mission – and Bond had to run for cover!

A concealed button caused hovercraft controls to drop into position

Hovercraft skirt

THE "BONDOLA"
At the press of a button, Q's gondola converted into a turbo-powered hovercraft. It helped 007 escape pursuit on the Venice canals during the *Moonraker* mission.

Bond takes a short cut across Venice's St Mark's Square

A NICE SET OF PIPES
When Q moved his workshop to a Scottish castle for *The World Is Not Enough* mission, he was moved to create a set of rocket-firing bagpipes.

Missile

Cast is hinged for reloading and maintenance

GHETTO-BLASTER
Not being a pop-music fan, Bond never found a use for Q's Ghetto Blaster. It typified Q's genius for concealing weapons in everyday objects.

Launcher

Firing button

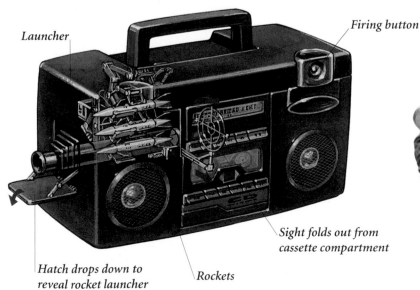

Sight folds out from cassette compartment

Hatch drops down to reveal rocket launcher

Rockets

LEG PULL
Even Bond was astonished when Q demonstrated this missile launcher, concealed in a plaster cast.

A WORLD OF SPIES

BOND'S MI6 ACTIVITIES have brought him into contact with many of the world's secret services, particularly US and Russian intelligence. The American CIA's vast resources have often come to his aid, and one of its top agents, Felix Leiter, remains a close friend. The Russian KGB has frequently been an enemy. However, along with other countries' secret services, it has sometimes "got into bed" with MI6 in the face of dire threats to world security posed by organized crime or by various lone megalomaniacs.

KGB badge

QUARREL
An easy-going Jamaican fisherman and CIA agent, he assisted 007 on the *Dr. No* mission.

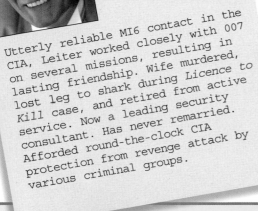

LEITER, FELIX
Service: CIA
Rank: N/A
Status: Retired
Security risk: Low

Utterly reliable MI6 contact in the CIA, Leiter worked closely with 007 on several missions, resulting in lasting friendship. Wife murdered, lost leg to shark during *Licence to Kill* case, and retired from active service. Now a leading security consultant. Has never remarried. Afforded round-the-clock CIA protection from revenge attack by various criminal groups.

JACK WADE
This likeable CIA agent was 007's contact during the *GoldenEye* and *Tomorrow Never Dies* missions. Enjoys ruffling 007's feathers by calling him "Jimbo".

HOLLY GOODHEAD
A CIA agent and rocket scientist, she worked with 007 on the *Moonraker* mission. Her ability to fly a space shuttle was particularly useful.

VIVE LA DIFFERENCE
This French agent helped 007 eliminate SPECTRE hit man Jacques Boitier prior to the *Thunderball* mission. Her identity remains a mystery – even to 007.

Rapelling wrist hook

WAI LIN
With her martial arts expertise, this Red Chinese agent was an invaluable ally for 007 on the *Tomorrow Never Dies* mission.

TIGER TANAKA
The Japanese security chief helped 007 defeat SPECTRE on the *You Only Live Twice* mission. Unusally for someone in his position, he also took part in dangerous undercover field work.

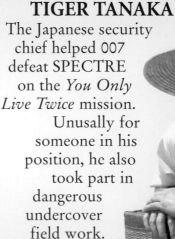

ERIC KRIEGLER
A typically ruthless
product of KGB
training, Kriegler was
eliminated by 007
during the *For Your
Eyes Only* mission.

ZORIN, MAX
Service: **ex-KGB**
Rank: **Unknown**
Status: **Deceased**
Security risk: **Nil**

KGB agent and
industrialist; the
psychotic product of a
Nazi genetic experiment
to create a master race.
Quit KGB and tried to
destroy US computer
industry. Eliminated by
007 during the *A View To
A Kill* mission.

AMASOVA, ANYA
Service: **KGB**
Rank: **Major**
Status: **Active
field agent**
Security risk:
Medium to high

Tough and resourceful KGB agent,
despite angelic appearance.
Formed unusually close working
relationship with 007 during *The
Spy Who Loved Me* joint MI6/KGB
mission, and played a full part
in Karl Stromberg's defeat.
Presumed to be still on active
service; area of operations
unknown.

GENERAL GOGOL

At times a dangerous enemy
at others a generous ally, the
KGB chief retains a healthy
respect for MI6, and 007 in
particular. A power-broker
in government circles, his
only weakness is a
penchant for beautiful
women – and the fear
his wife will one
day find out.

*In gratitude for
killing Zorin, Gogol
presented 007
with the Order of*

ORLOV
Service:
Soviet Red Army
Rank: **General**
Status: **Deceased**
Security risk:
Nil

Unstable, treacherous warmonger.
Attempted to destroy East-West
détente by staging nuclear
"accident". Claimed to be driven
by national pride but more likely
motivated by self-aggrandisement.
Shot near East German border by
Soviet troops while apparently
escaping to West with cache of
jewels stolen from Kremlin.

MAFIA MAN
Motivated
by greed
and self-interest,
Valentin Zukovsky
left the KGB and
set himself up as a Russian
mafia boss. Despite his criminal
activities, the roguish Zukovsky
assisted 007 on the *GoldenEye* and
The World Is Not Enough missions.

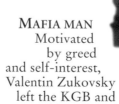

SUPERVILLAIN

Scar of
unknown origin

Military-
style suit

ERNST STAVRO BLOFELD –
the name still casts a chill at
MI6. As head of SPECTRE,
he masterminded several of the
gravest threats late-20th-century
civilization faced. Without Bond's
intervention, there is no doubt this
archfiend's dreams of world
domination would have come true.
Bond's pursuit of Blofeld, who
frequently resorted to plastic surgery
to change his appearance, was at great
personal cost: many of 007's friends and
lovers died at SPECTRE's hands – even
his own wife. To this day, nobody knows
if Blofeld is dead or planning some
new outrage.

THE MASTERMIND
Bond tracked Blofeld down
during the *You Only Live
Twice* mission. Coming face
to face with the master of
terror was an unnerving
experience – even for MI6's
toughest agent.

WASTE DISPOSAL
SPECTRE agents lived in fear
of their chief's inventive
methods of punishing failure
or betrayal, which included
a pool of piranhas (right)
and an exploding
chair (below).

*Blofeld's only love - apart
from power – was a white
Persian cat that sported a
diamond-studded collar*

THE MANY FACES OF ERNST
One of Blofeld's most cunning *coups* occurred during Bond's *Diamonds Are Forever* mission, when he both altered his appearance and created doubles of himself. Fortunately 007 was not fooled for long.

LOOKING GOOD
Blofeld assumed his most persuasive guise posing as a doctor eager to gain a title – a scheme 007 scotched on the *OHMSS* mission.

SPECTRE
The initials of the organization founded by Ernst Stavro Blofeld stood for The Special Executive for Counterintelligence, Terrorism, Revenge, and Extortion. One by one Bond defeated its agents, forcing Blofeld out of the shadows and into a personal showdown with 007.

RING OF EVIL
Top operatives of SPECTRE – and Blofeld himself – could sometimes be recognized by a distinctive octopus ring, which symbolized the organization's tentacular reach into the murkiest depths of world crime.

ATTACK ON 007
A routine helicopter flight turned nasty when the pilot was electrocuted. Control of the aircraft was taken over by a bald man in a wheelchair on a rooftop far below, who seemed to know Bond very well indeed.

CCTV screen allowed assassin to watch 007's struggle to survive

DOWN, DOWN
After a terrifying ride, 007 managed to break the remote control connection. He took over the helicopter himself, scooped up the assassin, and dropped him down a disused factory chimney. Could the man have been Ernst Stavro himself?

FOREVER APART
When Blofeld and his sidekick Irma Bunt gunned down Bond's wife, Teresa, on her wedding day, the duel between the mastermind and MI6's top agent became a full-blown vendetta.

Helicopter's remote controls on wheelchair fascia

23

THE MISSIONS

James Bond seldom mentions his MI6 assignments
– except to crack the occasional joke about an
enemy's personal foible or a femme fatale's exotic
stratagem. However, MI6 has not been so reticent,
and has thrown open its files and provided details
of all 007's most successful missions: the villains –
and lovers – he has encountered; the incredible
vehicles and other equipment issued to him by
Q Branch; the labyrinthine lairs he has penetrated
and destroyed; and some of the most amazing
pursuits and battles he has ever taken part in on
behalf of Her Majesty's Secret Service.

DR. NO

AN MI6 AGENT, John Strangways, was missing in Jamaica and Bond was sent to investigate. He discovered that Strangways was on the track of a certain Dr No, owner of a mine on the nearby island of Crab Key. The locals avoided Crab Key, believing it haunted. Bond landed there, but instead of spooks, encountered a girl named Honey on the beach. He was soon entangled in a deadly battle of wits with Dr No, who planned to destroy the entire US space programme.

QUARREL
This brave CIA agent took Bond to Crab Key, but was burned to death by Dr No's Dragon Tank.

Honey's shells fetched good prices on the US mainland

THREE BLIND MICE
Dr No's assassins posed as blind men to murder MI6's John Strangways as he left Kingston's exclusive Queen's Club.

NEXT HIT
Strangway's secretary was the Three Blind Mice's next target. She was gunned down before she could radio MI6 in London about Dr No's activities.

Hunting knife for cutting free shells

HONEY RYDER
Concealed on the beach at Crab Key, Bond could hardly believe his eyes when a girl arose, like Venus, from the waves. "Looking for shells?" asked Honey Ryder, fearing a competitor in the sea-shell trade. "No, I'm just looking," Bond replied.

Scuba-diver's mask

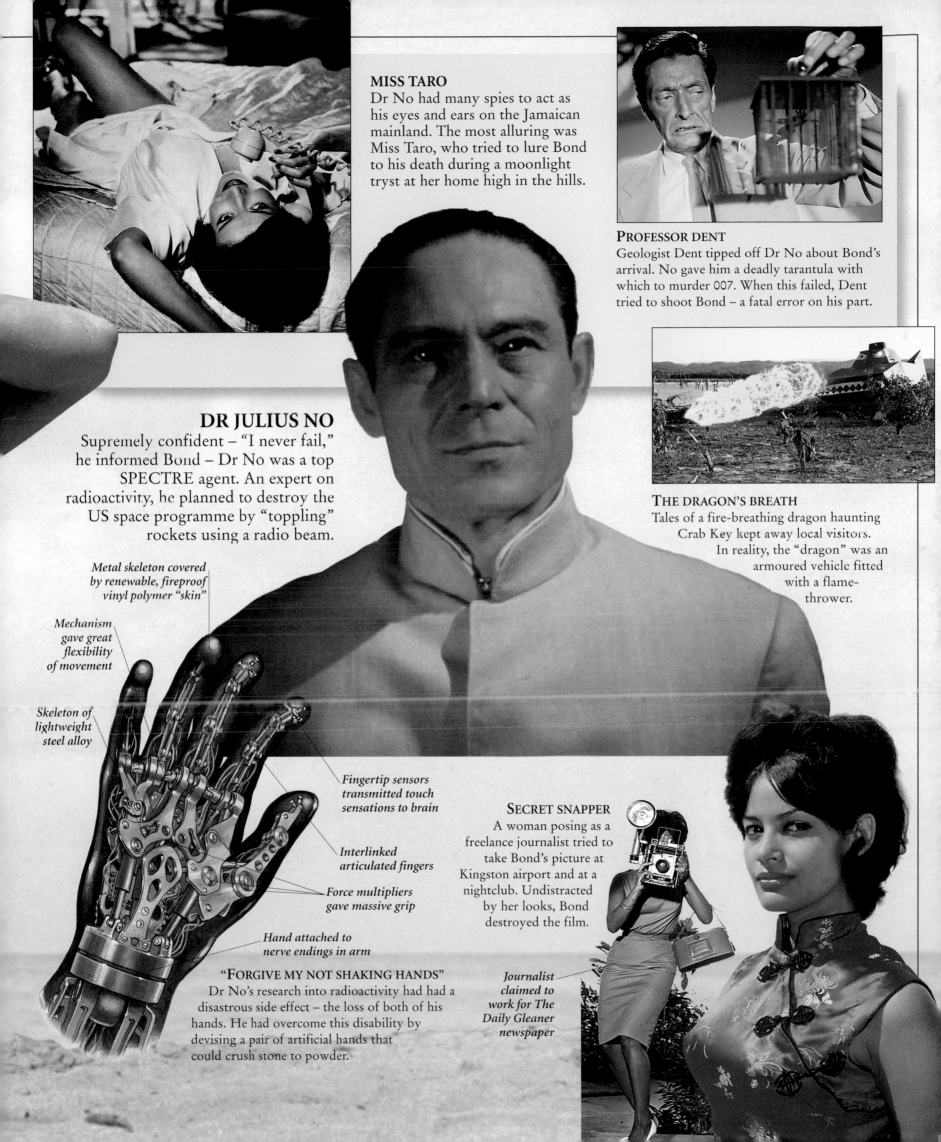

MISS TARO

Dr No had many spies to act as his eyes and ears on the Jamaican mainland. The most alluring was Miss Taro, who tried to lure Bond to his death during a moonlight tryst at her home high in the hills.

PROFESSOR DENT

Geologist Dent tipped off Dr No about Bond's arrival. No gave him a deadly tarantula with which to murder 007. When this failed, Dent tried to shoot Bond – a fatal error on his part.

DR JULIUS NO

Supremely confident – "I never fail," he informed Bond – Dr No was a top SPECTRE agent. An expert on radioactivity, he planned to destroy the US space programme by "toppling" rockets using a radio beam.

THE DRAGON'S BREATH

Tales of a fire-breathing dragon haunting Crab Key kept away local visitors. In reality, the "dragon" was an armoured vehicle fitted with a flame-thrower.

Metal skeleton covered by renewable, fireproof vinyl polymer "skin"

Mechanism gave great flexibility of movement

Skeleton of lightweight steel alloy

Fingertip sensors transmitted touch sensations to brain

Interlinked articulated fingers

Force multipliers gave massive grip

Hand attached to nerve endings in arm

SECRET SNAPPER

A woman posing as a freelance journalist tried to take Bond's picture at Kingston airport and at a nightclub. Undistracted by her looks, Bond destroyed the film.

"FORGIVE MY NOT SHAKING HANDS"

Dr No's research into radioactivity had had a disastrous side effect – the loss of both of his hands. He had overcome this disability by devising a pair of artificial hands that could crush stone to powder.

Journalist claimed to work for The Daily Gleaner newspaper

DR. NO'S LAIR

▲ **1.** *ONE WAY OUT*
Bond used his shoe to short circuit an electrified grill in his cell. He crawled into the network of pipes used to cool Crab Key's nuclear reactor.

CAPTURED BY DR NO'S GUARDS and locked in a cell, Bond knew that time was fast running out for himself and the beautiful, innocent Honey Ryder. Dr No's plan to eliminate them both and also destroy the American space programme appeared unstoppable – unless he could somehow get free. The feat pushed 007 to the limits of his ingenuity and endurance as he overcame an electrified barrier, blistering heat and near drowning to reach the nerve centre of Dr No's Crab Key lair.

DR NO
Encased in a protective suit and seated at the operations console at Crab Key, Dr No lived out his dreams of world domination.

◄ **2.** *LONG WAY DOWN*
The shaft dropped vertically some 7 metres (22 ft), and Bond jumped down. Landing skills acquired while learning to parachute jump helped him escape injury.

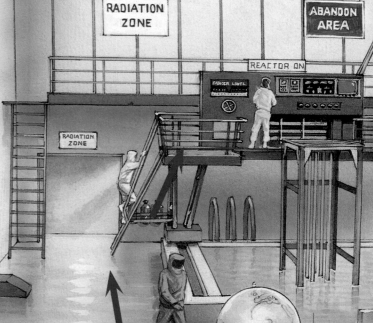

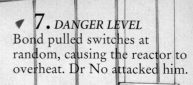

▼ **7.** *DANGER LEVEL*
Bond pulled switches at random, causing the reactor to overheat. Dr No attacked him.

RADIATION ZONE

ABANDON AREA

REACTOR ON

RADIATION ZONE

Heavy water

World globe

3. *BURNING METAL* ▶
He crawled out into a ventilator shaft. The metal grew hotter and hotter. Bond tore his jacket and shirt to make protective bandages for his hands and knees.

▲ **6.** *DEMOLITION MAN*
In disguise, Bond moved purposefully towards the reactor's cooling system, ignoring Dr No's order: "Get back to your post!"

◄ **4.** *RUSHING WATER*
As Bond crawled on, he heard a rumbling sound. The next moment a torrent of water knocked him flat. He held a single, lung-bursting breath until the wave had passed.

◄ **5.** *SUITED-UP*
The shaft led to Crab Key's decontamination area. Bond overpowered one of Dr No's guards and took his radiation-proof protective suit.

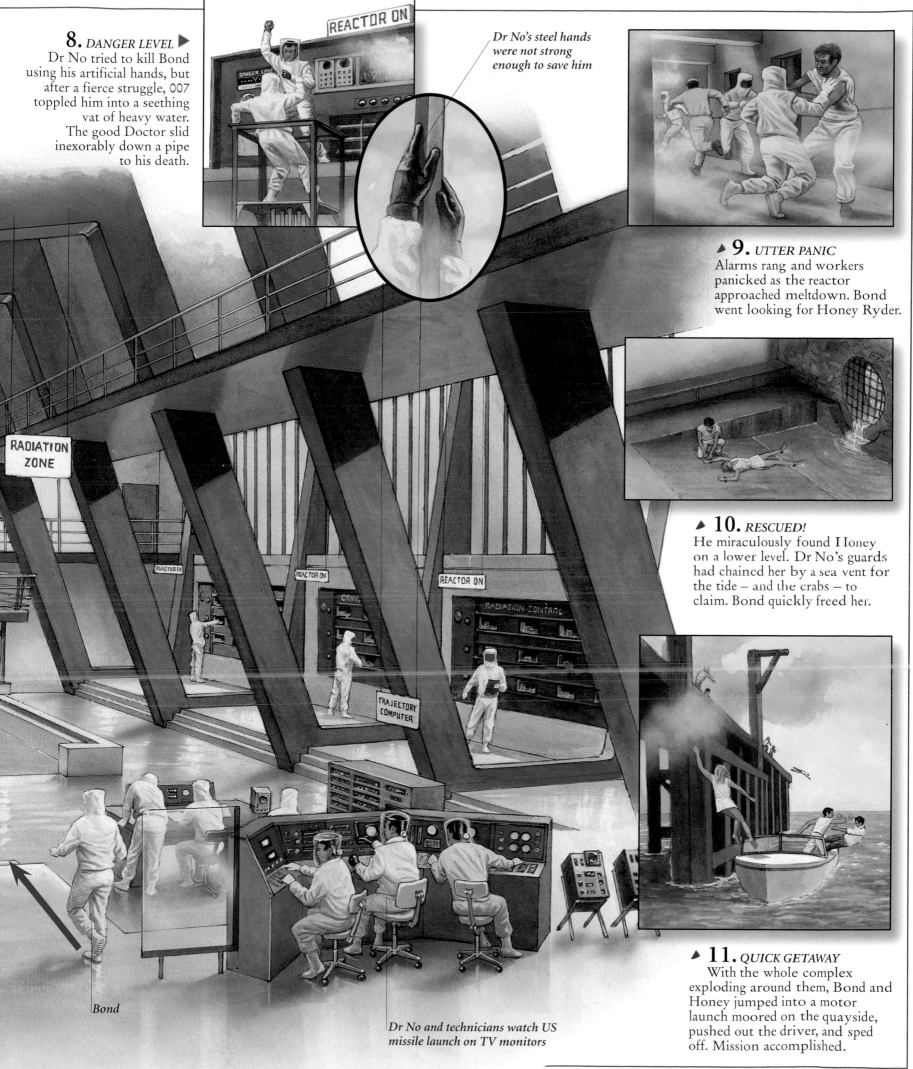

8. *DANGER LEVEL* ▶
Dr No tried to kill Bond using his artificial hands, but after a fierce struggle, 007 toppled him into a seething vat of heavy water. The good Doctor slid inexorably down a pipe to his death.

Dr No's steel hands were not strong enough to save him

▲ **9.** *UTTER PANIC*
Alarms rang and workers panicked as the reactor approached meltdown. Bond went looking for Honey Ryder.

▲ **10.** *RESCUED!*
He miraculously found Honey on a lower level. Dr No's guards had chained her by a sea vent for the tide – and the crabs – to claim. Bond quickly freed her.

▲ **11.** *QUICK GETAWAY*
With the whole complex exploding around them, Bond and Honey jumped into a motor launch moored on the quayside, pushed out the driver, and sped off. Mission accomplished.

RADIATION ZONE

Bond

Dr No and technicians watch US missile launch on TV monitors

FROM RUSSIA WITH LOVE

AN EXTRAORDINARY LETTER arrived at MI6 from a Russian cypher clerk in Istanbul. She claimed to have fallen in love with a photo of Bond in the office files. She wanted to defect and would bring a top-secret decoder, the Lektor, with her, on condition that Bond escorted her to England. It was an obvious trap, but M felt the prize of a Lektor was worth the risk. When 007 saw a photo of the cypher clerk, he thought the mission was worth the risk, too. Neither suspected the lengths to which SPECTRE would go to eliminate Bond and discredit the Service.

INNOCENT VICTIM

SPECTRE's plot to kill 007 and embroil MI6 in a sex scandal began when Russian cypher clerk Tanya Romanova became an unwitting pawn in the game. "Hmm – you're a fine-looking girl," observed villainous Rosa Klebb, formerly a KGB Colonel, now a top SPECTRE agent.

TATIANA ROMANOVA

Known to her friends as "Tanya", Tatiana trained as a ballerina before joining Soviet Intelligence. Believing herself on a KGB mission, she was smuggled into Bond's hotel room, where their encounter was secretly filmed by SPECTRE agents. She fell in love with Bond for real as, posing as Mr and Mrs Somerset, they escaped on the *Orient Express* to Venice with the Lektor decoder.

KERIM BEY

Bond's ally in Istanbul was Kerim Bey, head of MI6's Station T. Bond's arrival shattered Bey's calm existence, for SPECTRE began to stir up trouble between Bey's men and the Russians. Bey had his girlfriend to thank for escaping a bomb attack on his headquarters.

A black velvet choker was all Tanya needed to attract 007

Kerim Bey: under fire at the camp

GANG OF FOUR

The plot to ensnare Bond was the brainchild of chess-master Kronsteen. Rosa Klebb's role, in addition to recruiting Tatiana, was to brief Bond's killer, escaped convict and homicidal paranoiac Donald "Red" Grant. He had been primed by Morzeny, head of SPECTRE's training school.

ORDERS TO KILL
"Let his death be a particularly unpleasant and humiliating one," SPECTRE chief Ernst Stavro Blofeld instructed Rosa Klebb, Kronsteen and Morzeny. The gang was sure that Bond would soon pay dearly for meddling in SPECTRE's affairs.

KILLING MACHINE
Klebb inspected Grant (left), while visiting the school (right).

GYPSY CAMP BATTLE
Kerim Bey appeared to be the prime target when the gypsy camp was attacked by Russians led by the KGB's top assassin Krilencu. Bey took a bullet in the shoulder during the gun battle and 007 himself only emerged unscathed because of the intervention of a mysterious blond man. The battle won, Bond settled the gypsy girls' love-wrangle in his own, non-violent way.

THE "GYPSY WAY"
Bey took Bond to visit the local gypsies. At the camp they witnessed a battle between two girls in love with the same man. Before the affair could be settled "in the gypsy way" - by one girl killing the other – shots rang out.

CAN I DO YOU NOW, SIR?
When SPECTRE's plan to kill Bond failed, Klebb took matters into her own hands. Posing as a maid, she pulled a gun as Bond and Tanya relaxed in their Venice hotel. Bond disarmed her, but she was not finished yet...

LASHING OUT
Klebb's shoe concealed a flick-knife coated with a deadly poison. Tanya shot her just in time. "She had her kicks," remarked James Bond.

Poisoned blade: lethal within 7 seconds

BOX OF TRICKS

JUST BEFORE BOND LEFT for Istanbul he was issued by Q with a black leather briefcase. It looked ordinary, but, hidden in secret compartments were 40 rounds of ammunition, a throwing knife and 50 gold sovereigns. The case also contained a sniper's rifle and a talcum powder tin fitted with a tear-gas cartridge, which was triggered by the case's catches. "A nasty little Christmas present," Bond observed, "but I shouldn't think I'll need it on this assignment." How wrong could he be!

Queen Elizabeth II

GOLD SOVEREIGNS
At the back of the case were two straps each containing 25 gold sovereigns. Handy for unforeseen travelling expenses – or bribing one's way out of trouble.

Talc in top compartment

Coins attached to plastic strip

Charge blows top off canister

Tear-gas canister

Sensor

TALCUM BOMB
The talc tin concealed two tear-gas canisters. The magnetic sensor was triggered by the case's catches.

.25 ammo for AR-7 rifle

Stud unscrews

AMMO TUBES
The spine of the case contained two hollow tubes, each holding 20 rounds of ammunition.

CONCEALED WEAPON
A button near one of the catches releases a flat throwing knife from the front of the case.

Button releases spring mechanism

HERE'S THE CATCH
Q explained that if the case was opened in the normal way, by moving the catches to the side, the tear-gas cartridge would explode. To prevent this, the catches had to be turned horizontally, then opened.

Safety cut-out switch

Magnetic sensor linked to gas canister

Safety-catch arm

Detonator lever

Trigger switch fires gas if cut-out switch not activated

Turning catch 90° operates arm to activate safety switch; pushing catch outwards then opens case safely

Armed   *Disarmed*

Tanya's drink was spiked with chloral hydrate

SOMETHING FISHY...
Dinner on the Orient Express: present were Bond, Tanya, and a certain Captain Nash of MI6, who displayed an odd preference for red wine with fish, and whose smugness grated on Bond. A moment later Tanya fainted – her wine had been drugged.

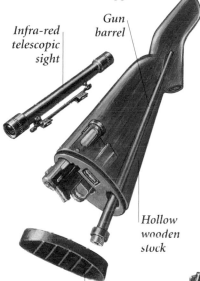

Infra-red telescopic sight

Gun barrel

Hollow wooden stock

Butt-end comes off to reveal rifle parts

AR7 RIFLE
The components of this sniper's rifle fitted snugly into the hollow stock. The gun's infra-red sight proved invaluable for night work, such as the assassination of Bulgarian hit man Krilencu. He was shot by Kerim Bey while trying to sneak from a hideout concealed by a film poster.

THE CASE IS OPENED
"Red wine with fish – that should have told me something," mused Bond as "Captain Nash", alias SPECTRE assassin Red Grant, pulled a gun, seized the Lektor decoder and announced that he would shoot Bond "slowly". 007 had just his wits and briefcase to rely on. The case's gold sovereigns tempted Grant. He opened it, the tear-gas bomb exploded in his face, and Bond seized his chance to attack.

Piano-wire garotte

Coil of wire

TIME IS TIGHT
Grant's favourite weapon was a wristwatch whose winder pulled out to become a wire garotte. During their final battle on the train, Bond managed to use this lethal weapon on Grant himself.

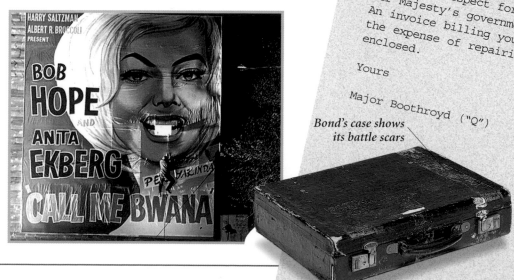

Bond's case shows its battle scars

Q's face shows his disappointment

GOLDFINGER

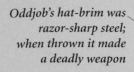

A CROOKED CARD GAME, a bump on the head and a beautiful, dead girl covered in gold paint were Bond's macabre introduction to one of his most formidable adversaries, Auric Goldfinger. MI6 suspected Goldfinger of smuggling vast quantities of gold bullion around the world. Armed with a bar of gold as bait, Bond was assigned to uncover the truth about the man with the "Midas touch".

CARD CHEAT
In Miami, Bond rumbled Goldfinger's lucrative scheme to cheat Simmons, a rich American, at gin rummy. He ordered Goldfinger to start losing – to the tune of $15,000!

GOLDEN GIRL
Jill Masterson played a part in Goldfinger's card scam, until Bond walked into her life. She immediately dumped her loathsome boss, but paid dearly for a night with 007. She died of skin suffocation after being painted gold.

Part of a Nazi hoard missing since World War II

NAZI TREASURE
Goldfinger challenged Bond to a round of golf. The prize: MI6's bar of Nazi gold, worth £5,000. Bond soon found that Goldfinger was up to his cheating tricks again, but outfoxed him on the vital 18th hole.

TILLY MASTERSON
Someone else, apart from James Bond, was interested in Goldfinger's movements. Jill Masterson's sister, Tilly, was out for revenge for her sister's death. She took a shot at Goldfinger when he stopped on a mountain road, but missed. Bond later encountered her when spying out Goldfinger's factory, and they joined forces for a while. Tragically, tough-talking Tilly fell victim to a cruel blow from Oddjob's hat.

THE GOLDEN ROLLS-ROYCE
Bond tracked Goldfinger's Rolls to the villain's factory, Auric Enterprises, in Switzerland. The complex was protected by cameras, trip wires, and guards. Bond soon discovered how Goldfinger smuggled gold: it was hidden within panels in his car; sections of the bodywork were also made of gold and sprayed with paint.

Formal attire added to his air of menace

CUTTING REMARK

After a car chase around Goldfinger's factory, Bond was captured and strapped to a gold table. Gold was Goldfinger's obsession: "All my life I have been in love with its colour, its brilliance, its divine heaviness..." Above Bond's head loomed an industrial laser. "Do you expect me to talk?" Bond shouted as the laser beam moved towards his groin. "No, Mr Bond," Goldfinger replied. "I expect you to die!" Bond blurted out a phrase he had overheard, "Operation Grand Slam". Suddenly Goldfinger decided that 007 was more use to him alive.

Goldfinger's laser cut through solid metal

HOODS' CONVENTION

Goldfinger outlined Operation Grand Slam to America's most powerful crime barons – who, unknowingly, had all contributed to it. Then he had them murdered.

MASTER AND SERVANT

Goldfinger's criminal career had brought him fabulous wealth. His possessions included numerous business interests, one of the finest stud farms in the US, a golf club, a vintage Rolls-Royce and Oddjob, a mute Korean manservant. Immensely strong and a karate expert, Oddjob was utterly loyal and relished doing his master's dirty work.

IMMUNE TO BOND

When Bond tried to turn on the charm with Pussy, she gave him the old heave-ho – at first, at least.

PUSSY GALORE

Goldfinger's most attractive associate was ace pilot and judo expert Pussy Galore. Bond realized that if he was to have any chance of uncovering and foiling Operation Grand Slam, Goldfinger's masterplan, he had to get her on his side.

THE BONDMOBILE

SILVER MACHINE
The Aston Martin DB5 put 007 in the driving seat in his fight against supervillains like Goldfinger.

ALTHOUGH 007 is notoriously careless with the equipment issued to him, there is one item that retains a close hold on his affections – the superb Aston Martin DB5 entrusted to him on the *Goldfinger* mission. A truly lethal combination of beauty and power, the DB5 came equipped with an eye-popping array of weaponry and equipment, including machine guns, tyre slashers, a bulletproof shield, a radar screen for tracking enemy vehicles and, most remarkable of all, an ejector seat for the removal of unwanted passengers. Bond wrote-off the car during a high-speed chase with Goldfinger's henchmen, but Q Branch later recovered and repaired it for Bond's personal use.

Flap rose to reveal screen

Ground-glass radar screen

Main control console hidden beneath padded arm rest

AT THE WHEEL
A bank of switches next to the driver operated the defence systems. The dashboard had a radar screen for tracking enemy vehicles using a pre-planted homing device.

Telephone handset concealed in door panel

ASTON MARTIN DB5:
SPECIFICATIONS

- **Max. speed:** 145.2 mph (232.3 km/h)
- **Acceleration:** 0–60 mph (0–96 km/h) in 7.1 seconds
- **Fuel consumption** (fast cruising): 17.3 mpg
- **Length:** 179.8 in (4567 mm)
- **Width:** 66.5 in (1689 mm)
- **Engine capacity:** 3995 cc

Radar scanner hidden behind racing mirror

.30 calibre Browning machine gun behind each sidelight

Hydraulic overrider

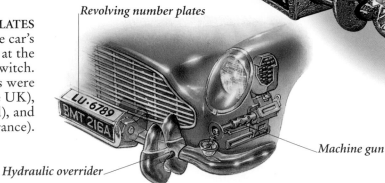

Revolving number plates

NUMBER PLATES
To confuse pursuers, the car's number plates revolved at the flick of a switch. The licence plates were BMT 216A (valid in the UK), LU 6789 (Switzerland), and 4711-EA-62 (France).

Hydraulic overrider

Machine gun

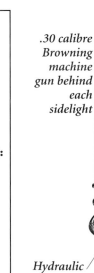

RAM RAIDER
The front of the DB5 packed a real punch: the bumpers had hydraulic overriders that could be used as battering rams, and twin Browning machine guns were concealed behind the front indicators.

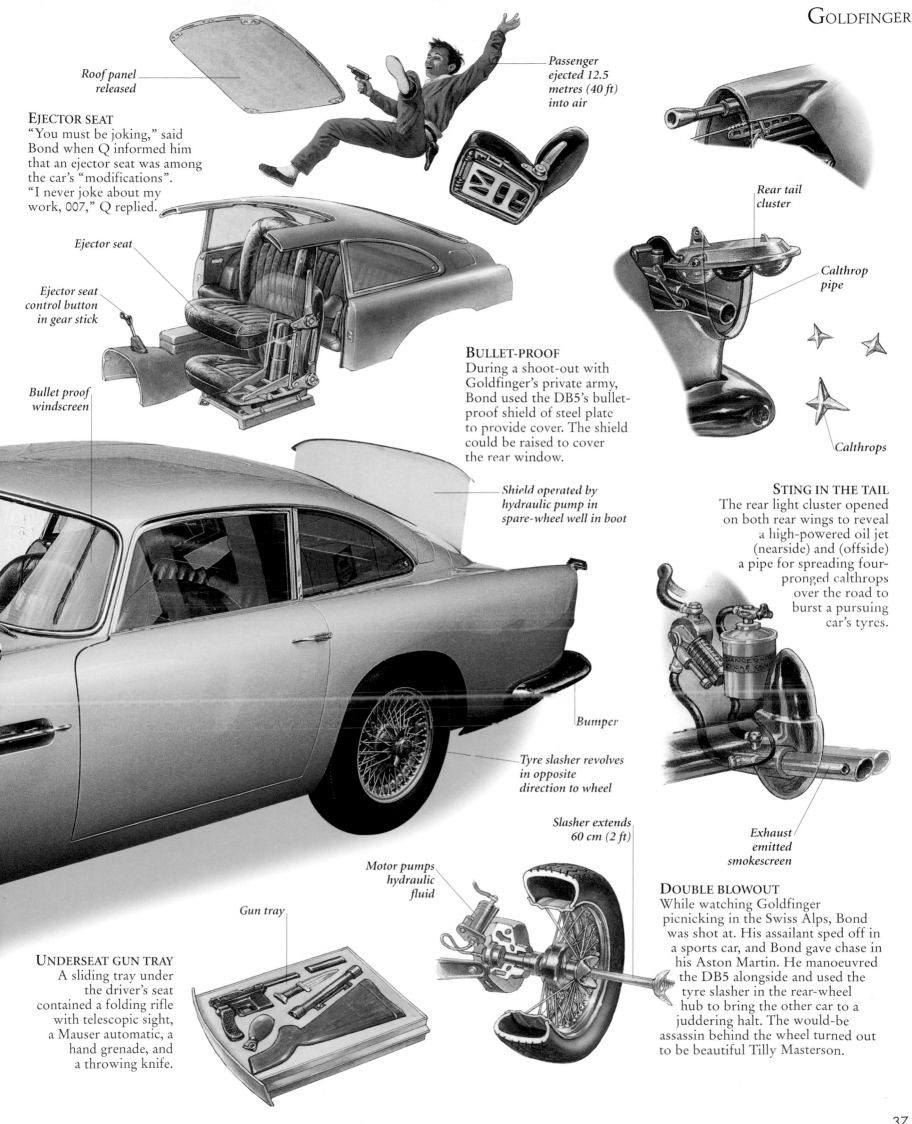

Roof panel released

EJECTOR SEAT
"You must be joking," said Bond when Q informed him that an ejector seat was among the car's "modifications". "I never joke about my work, 007," Q replied.

Passenger ejected 12.5 metres (40 ft) into air

Ejector seat

Ejector seat control button in gear stick

Rear tail cluster

Calthrop pipe

Bullet proof windscreen

BULLET-PROOF
During a shoot-out with Goldfinger's private army, Bond used the DB5's bullet-proof shield of steel plate to provide cover. The shield could be raised to cover the rear window.

Calthrops

Shield operated by hydraulic pump in spare-wheel well in boot

STING IN THE TAIL
The rear light cluster opened on both rear wings to reveal a high-powered oil jet (nearside) and (offside) a pipe for spreading four-pronged calthrops over the road to burst a pursuing car's tyres.

Bumper

Tyre slasher revolves in opposite direction to wheel

Slasher extends 60 cm (2 ft)

Exhaust emitted smokescreen

Motor pumps hydraulic fluid

Gun tray

DOUBLE BLOWOUT
While watching Goldfinger picnicking in the Swiss Alps, Bond was shot at. His assailant sped off in a sports car, and Bond gave chase in his Aston Martin. He manoeuvred the DB5 alongside and used the tyre slasher in the rear-wheel hub to bring the other car to a juddering halt. The would-be assassin behind the wheel turned out to be beautiful Tilly Masterson.

UNDERSEAT GUN TRAY
A sliding tray under the driver's seat contained a folding rifle with telescopic sight, a Mauser automatic, a hand grenade, and a throwing knife.

OPERATION GRAND SLAM

▲ 1. GAS ATTACK
Pussy Galore's Flying Circus released nerve gas, eliminating troops.

GOLDFINGER'S MASTERPLAN, Operation Grand Slam, was typically outrageous: to break into the US Gold Bullion Depository at Fort Knox and explode a nuclear bomb in its vaults. The entire US gold reserve of $15 billion would be contaminated with radioactivity, increasing the value of Goldfinger's own gold hoard tenfold. With a laser to cut a way in, a squadron of planes – Pussy Galore's Flying Circus – to neutralize troops in the area with nerve gas, and his own armed force, Goldfinger was confident of success. "You will be there to see for yourself," he said to Bond. "Too closely for comfort, I'm afraid."

2. EXPLOSIVE ENTRANCE
Goldfinger's troops travelled unopposed down Bullion Boulevard. The main gates to Fort Knox were quickly blown open.

Fort Knox: constructed from Tennessee granite

Goldfinger's men were hidden in US Army trucks

Bullion Boulevard

Main gates

Perimeter fence: wrought iron set in concrete

Laser mounted on ambulance

The "largest bank in the world" contained $15 billion.

▲ 3. WIDE OPEN
With the bank's defenses destroyed, Goldfinger's troops drove through the gates and around to the loading area at the back.

4. FORCED ENTRY ▶
An industrial laser mounted on a US Army ambulance bored through the vault's steel doors.

Oddjob

At first, Bond was handcuffed to Oddjob

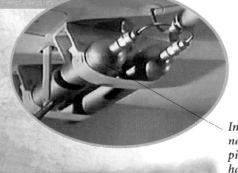

WHAT WENT WRONG...

The person directly responsible for Operation Grand Slam's failure was Goldfinger's pilot, Pussy Galore. Bond won her over to the side of good, and she switched the gas in her planes' canisters and tipped off the US government. "I must have appealed to her maternal side," mused Bond.

Goldfinger arrived in a Hiller UH-12E4 helicopter.

Instead of deadly nerve gas, Pussy's pilots released a harmless substance

SURPRISE ATTACK
As Goldfinger prepared to leave Bond to an explosive fate, the soldiers, who were only feigning death, launched a blistering surprise attack. Meanwhile, deep inside the bank vault, Bond managed to undo the handcuffs binding him to the bomb. But as the seconds ticked away, he was then faced by a fearsome adversary: Oddjob, Goldfinger's implacable manservant.

▶ **5.** *NUCLEAR BOMB*
Goldfinger arrived in a helicopter with the atomic device.

Pussy Galore

Nuclear device was cobalt and iodine

Nuclear device

Switch disarmed bomb

Oddjob "blew a fuse" battling Bond

ELECTRIC EXIT
No match for martial-arts expert Oddjob, Bond had to rely on his wits. As Oddjob reached out to retrieve his lethal, razor-brimmed hat, which was embedded in some steel bars, Bond seized a power line, broken during their struggle, and gave the fanatical flunky the shock of his life.

Timer

Atomic device enclosed in a steel box

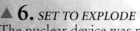
▲ **6.** *SET TO EXPLODE*
The nuclear device was placed inside the vault. Bond was handcuffed to it and the timer was set. 007 had just 4 minutes to live.

The timer showed just seven seconds to spare

BOMB DISPOSAL
At this stage in his career Bond lacked the technical know-how to disarm the bomb. Luckily, a US expert was on hand to flick the right switch.

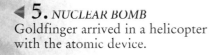

THUNDERBALL

A NATO VULCAN BOMBER carrying two atomic bombs had crashed in the Caribbean. To make a serious situation even more critical, SPECTRE then informed the British government that it had hijacked the plane's cargo. Unless a ransom of £100 million was paid in seven days, a major city in England or the US would be laid waste. MI6 called in all its top agents, but only one had a lead: James Bond. With four days to go, 007 flew to the Bahamas, where a femme fatale, a beautiful avenger, and a shark in human form called Emilio Largo awaited him.

SEVEN BELLS
Big Ben struck seven times at 6 pm as a sign of agreement to SPECTRE's terms.

DANGEROUS LIAISON
NATO pilot Major Derval had begun an affair with Fiona Volpe. She arranged his death so that a SPECTRE agent could impersonate him, kill the crew of his Vulcan bomber and ditch it in the Caribbean.

FIONA VOLPE
A SPECTRE executioner, Fiona orchestrated the Vulcan hijack and ensured unreliable colleagues were eliminated.

Fiona rode a rocket-firing BSA Lightning

WILD THING
"Do you like wild things, Mr Bond, James Bond?" asked Fiona. "You should be locked up in a cage," he replied.

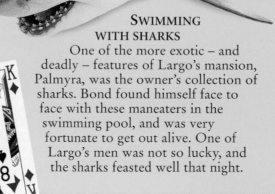

HOTEL KIDNAP
While Bond was busy with Domino at a carnival (right), Paula was seized by Fiona Volpe and Largo's men, led by Vargas.

PAULA CAPLAN
This MI6 agent gave her life to safeguard Bond's mission. He was too late to rescue her from Largo's home, Palmyra.

THE LAST DANCE
Bond discovered Paula's dead body at Largo's mansion. Back at his hotel, he found Fiona Volpe in his bath! She planned to seduce him and then watch him die in her arms as they danced. However, Bond swung her round to take the bullet meant for him.

DOMINO DERVAL

The sister of NATO pilot Major Derval, Domino was Largo's trophy girlfriend, lounging away her days at his mansion. She was tired of her "guardian's" overbearing ways and soon became attracted to Bond. Dislike of Largo turned to hatred when she learned that he had been behind her brother's death.

EMILIO LARGO

The piratical SPECTRE Number Two was the proud owner of a luxury yacht, a huge house, and a massive ego. He was also a bad loser – as Bond discovered when he beat him at *chemin de fer* during their first meeting at a local casino.

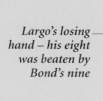

Largo's losing hand – his eight was beaten by Bond's nine

SWIMMING WITH SHARKS
One of the more exotic – and deadly – features of Largo's mansion, Palmyra, was the owner's collection of sharks. Bond found himself face to face with these maneaters in the swimming pool, and was very fortunate to get out alive. One of Largo's men was not so lucky, and the sharks feasted well that night.

VARGAS
Largo's pet assassin, Vargas, had no vices, except for killing people. He "got the point" when he tried to murder Bond and Domino.

DISCO VOLANTE

THE DOMINO EFFECT
Bond needed to find out if the bombs were on board the *Disco Volante*, and found an ally in Domino Derval, Largo's mistress. She wanted Largo killed for causing her brother's death.

MOORED OFF the coast of Bermuda, the *Disco Volante* appeared nothing more than the plaything of millionaire playboy Emilio Largo. But in reality, the 100-ton luxury yacht was a floating fortress, a pirate ship commanded by a bloodthirsty buccaneer. The vessel was crucial to SPECTRE's scheme to hijack two atomic bombs and detonate them unless the US government paid up.

Cannon

Sub recovery chamber

Main engine room:

A-bomb salvaged

Electronic doors in aluminium/magnesium-alloy hull allow secret launch of submarine.

Main propellers powered by two Daimler-Benz four-stroke supercharged engines

BOMB RECOVERY
Having caused the RAF Vulcan to crash into the sea, Emilio Largo, like a pirate of old, prepared to plunder its cargo – two atomic bombs.

Vulcan bomber concealed on the seabed beneath camouflage netting

SUB RECOVERY
Largo's men reached the bomber on motorized sleds.

ATOMIC BOMB SLED
Housed in the belly of the ship was a submarine, purpose-built to transport the bombs from the crashed bomber to the ship. The sled was equipped with headlights and armed with six forward-firing, high-velocity spearguns.

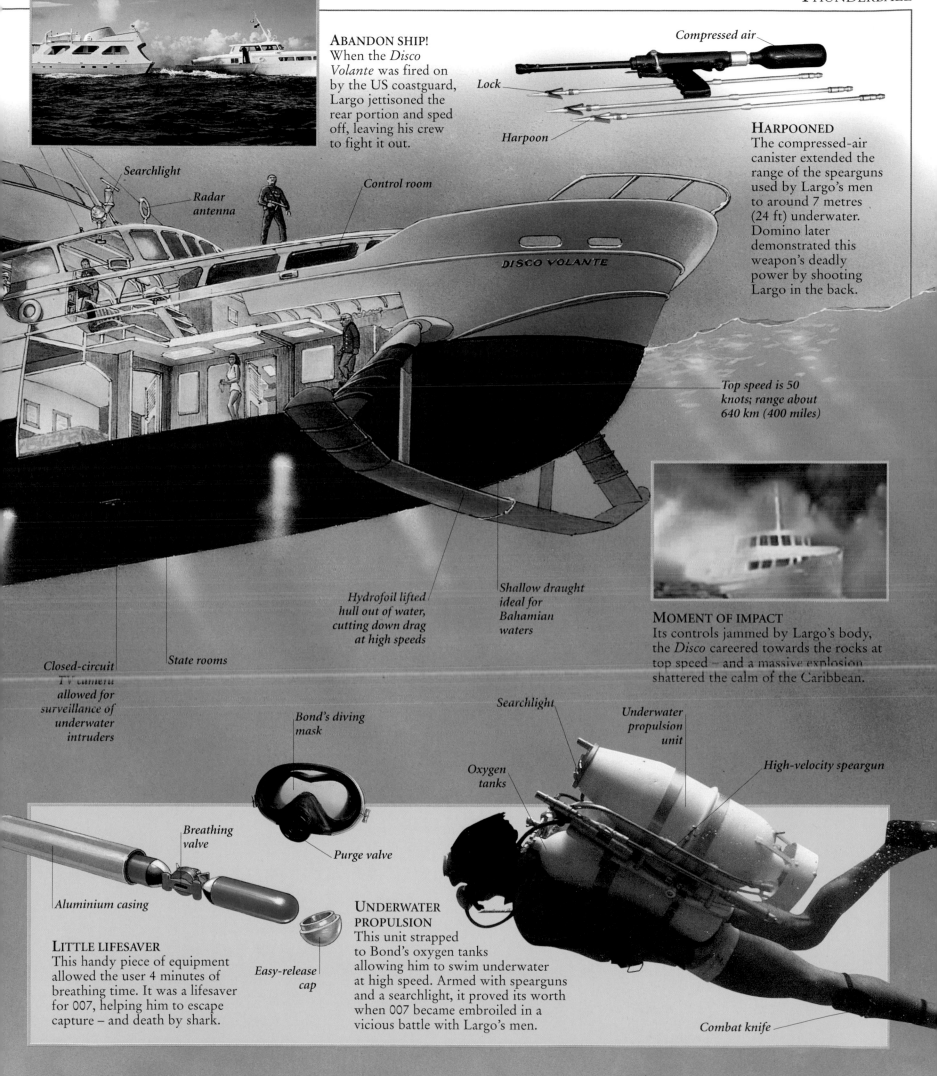

ABANDON SHIP!
When the *Disco Volante* was fired on by the US coastguard, Largo jettisoned the rear portion and sped off, leaving his crew to fight it out.

Compressed air

Lock

Harpoon

HARPOONED
The compressed-air canister extended the range of the spearguns used by Largo's men to around 7 metres (24 ft) underwater. Domino later demonstrated this weapon's deadly power by shooting Largo in the back.

Searchlight

Radar antenna

Control room

DISCO VOLANTE

Top speed is 50 knots; range about 640 km (400 miles)

Hydrofoil lifted hull out of water, cutting down drag at high speeds

Shallow draught ideal for Bahamian waters

MOMENT OF IMPACT
Its controls jammed by Largo's body, the *Disco* careered towards the rocks at top speed – and a massive explosion shattered the calm of the Caribbean.

Closed-circuit TV camera allowed for surveillance of underwater intruders

State rooms

Bond's diving mask

Searchlight

Underwater propulsion unit

Oxygen tanks

High-velocity speargun

Breathing valve

Purge valve

Aluminium casing

LITTLE LIFESAVER
This handy piece of equipment allowed the user 4 minutes of breathing time. It was a lifesaver for 007, helping him to escape capture – and death by shark.

Easy-release cap

UNDERWATER PROPULSION
This unit strapped to Bond's oxygen tanks allowing him to swim underwater at high speed. Armed with spearguns and a searchlight, it proved its worth when 007 became embroiled in a vicious battle with Largo's men.

Combat knife

YOU ONLY LIVE TWICE

BRITISH NAVAL COMMANDER MURDERED

HONG KONG
Commander James Bond of the British Navy was killed last night by unknown assailants. Assassins broke into apartment and shot him as he lay in bed. Neighbours reported hearing many sh...

007 RIP
Bond's death was reported in the Hong Kong press.

BOND'S SUCCESSES against SPECTRE had made him a marked man, and MI6 decided to fake his death to throw his enemies off the scent. Meanwhile, a US space capsule had been literally swallowed by another spacecraft over the Sea of Japan. The Americans suspected the Russians and threatened retaliation. With another US launch only weeks away, MI6 believed a third party was trying to foment nuclear war between the superpowers. Bond was dispatched to Tokyo, where, aided by the Japanese Secret Service, he infiltrated the headquarters of a corrupt industrialist. But 007's cover was blown by a scheming vixen and his "second life" was soon spiralling out of control.

Bird 1's doors opened like jaws

US space capsule

Bird 1 returned to base with US craft

Soviet insignia aroused US suspicions

Retractable legs extended for landing

BIRD 1
Launched from an unknown Far East location, Bird 1 had hijacked a US spacecraft. The US blamed Russia; the Russians protested their innocence.

AKI
Calm and assured, Aki was a top Japanese Secret Service agent who came to 007's aid more than once in her customized Toyota sports car. Their love-affair was tragically cut short by an assassin's poison.

Aki and Tiger introduced Bond to some of the intricacies of Japanese culture

TIGER TANAKA
The youthful head of the Japanese Secret Service, Tiger Tanaka forged a strong working relationship with Bond. The centres of his operation were an underground Tokyo HQ with its own metro train, an ancient castle, and a training school for his Ninja fighting force.

HELGA BRANDT
Mr Osato's Confidential Secretary also worked for SPECTRE, and was far more devious than her boss. She seduced 007 (not a very difficult task) then attempted to murder him in a plane crash. Once again, Blofeld showed no mercy when she failed.

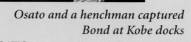

FISH FOOD
Blofeld's love of animals extended beyond his white Persian cat: he also kept piranhas. Helga Brandt discovered that his fishy friends, capable of stripping a person to a skeleton in minutes, were not just for show.

Osato and a henchman captured Bond at Kobe docks

MR OSATO
The chief of Osato Chemicals and Engineering, the company that supplied SPECTRE with liquid oxygen for rocket fuel, Mr Osato was ordered by Blofeld to kill Bond. The price of his failure was a bullet from Blofeld's gun.

ERNST STAVRO BLOFELD
Throughout Bond's career, the SPECTRE chief had lurked behind the scenes, masterminding horrific crimes and dispensing ruthless punishments to those who disappointed him. The *You Only Live Twice* mission revealed that evil had a human face.

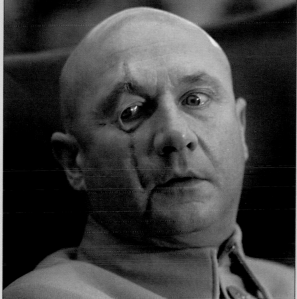

KISSY SUZUKI
One of Tiger Tanaka's top agents, the courageous Kissy managed to resist Bond's advances – at least until the mission was accomplished.

TURNING JAPANESE
In order to track down Blofeld, Bond had to go undercover. He was disguised as a Japanese fisherman and Tiger Tanaka found him a "bride" – in reality an agent called Kissy Suzuki. The pair then posed as peasants in a remote fishing community.

Kissy in traditional bridal costume

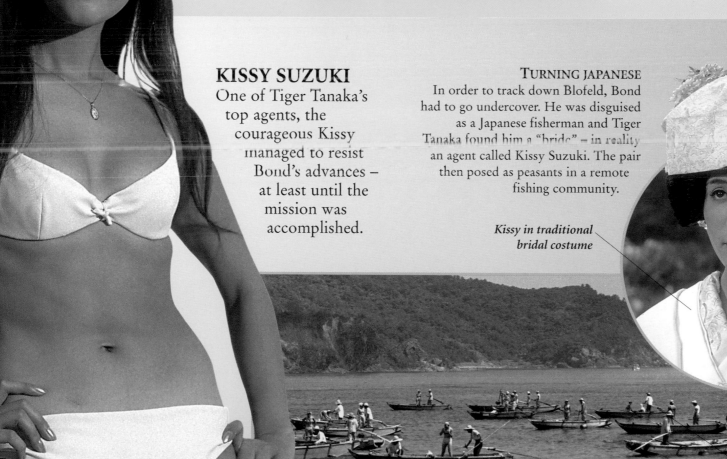

Bond and Kissy tried to blend in with the other fishermen.

LITTLE NELLIE

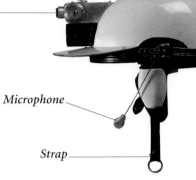

Rotor blade

BOND BELIEVED BLOFELD's lair was hidden in a volcano range on a remote Japanese island – but where? Q supplied 007 with the ideal vehicle for low-level aerial reconnaissance – an autogyro nicknamed "Little Nellie". This remarkable aircraft was fast, fuel-efficient, highly manoeuvrable, and could take off and land in a small space. She also had an arsenal of weapons to defend her "honour".

Cine camera

Microphone

Strap

PILOT'S EYE
A cine-camera sited in the helmet instantaneously transmitted a pilot's-eye view back to base.

HELMET

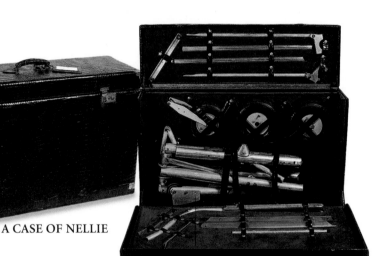

A CASE OF NELLIE

Air-frame parts fit snugly into each case

Windscreen

Static pressure head for air-speed indicator and altimeter

SPECIAL DELIVERY
One of Little Nellie's greatest assets was her portability. Her lightweight aluminium frame and fibreglass body was easily dismantled. The parts fitted into four crocodile-hide suitcases and could be easily transported anywhere in the world in a conventional airliner's hold. Once at the required destination, the parts could be quickly assembled by Q's team.

Pitot pressure head, sensing the pressure from forward speed

Machine gun

Little Nellie

LITTLE NELLIE:
SPECIFICATIONS

- **Max. speed:** 130 mph (208 km/h)
- **Acceleration:** 0–96 mph (0–154 km/h) in 12.5 secs
- **Altitude:** 5644 m (18,517 ft)
- **Fuel consumption:** 11.2 km/l
- **Length: fuselage:** 3.4 m (11 ft); rotor blades: 6.1 m (20 ft)
- **Width:** 1.6 m (5 ft 3 in)
- **Engine capacity:** 1634 cc

GUIDED MISSILES
The autogyro's deadliest weapons were two heat-seeking guided missiles that locked on to the heat generated by an enemy aircraft's engine.

Rocket packs

Missile

Nosewheel

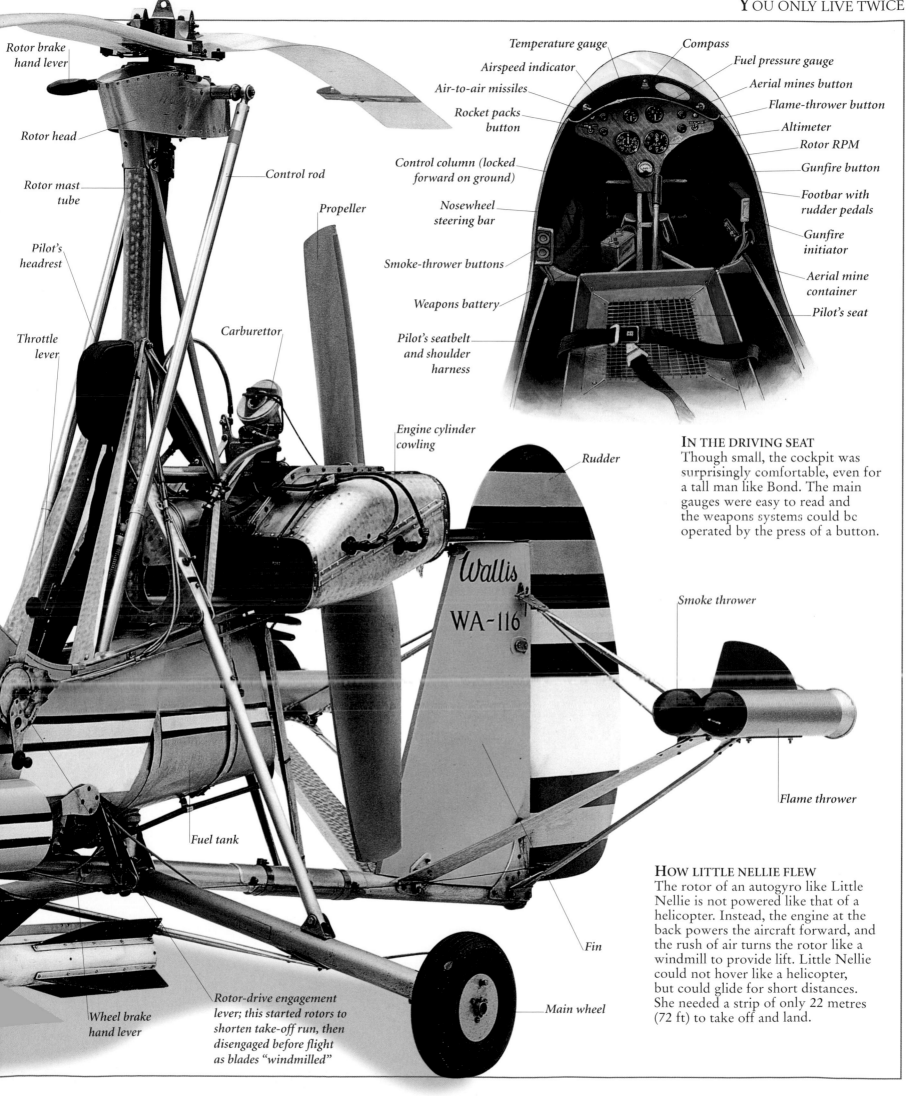

Rotor brake hand lever

Rotor head

Rotor mast tube

Control rod

Pilot's headrest

Throttle lever

Carburettor

Propeller

Temperature gauge

Airspeed indicator

Air-to-air missiles

Rocket packs button

Control column (locked forward on ground)

Nosewheel steering bar

Smoke-thrower buttons

Weapons battery

Pilot's seatbelt and shoulder harness

Compass

Fuel pressure gauge

Aerial mines button

Flame-thrower button

Altimeter

Rotor RPM

Gunfire button

Footbar with rudder pedals

Gunfire initiator

Aerial mine container

Pilot's seat

IN THE DRIVING SEAT
Though small, the cockpit was surprisingly comfortable, even for a tall man like Bond. The main gauges were easy to read and the weapons systems could be operated by the press of a button.

Engine cylinder cowling

Rudder

Smoke thrower

Flame thrower

Fuel tank

Wallis
WA-116

Wheel brake hand lever

Rotor-drive engagement lever; this started rotors to shorten take-off run, then disengaged before flight as blades "windmilled"

Fin

Main wheel

HOW LITTLE NELLIE FLEW
The rotor of an autogyro like Little Nellie is not powered like that of a helicopter. Instead, the engine at the back powers the aircraft forward, and the rush of air turns the rotor like a windmill to provide lift. Little Nellie could not hover like a helicopter, but could glide for short distances. She needed a strip of only 22 metres (72 ft) to take off and land.

VOLCANO ATTACK

A CAVE BENEATH a dormant volcano led Bond and Kissy Suzuki to discover Blofeld's lair, deep inside the volcano crater. From there, Blofeld planned to launch a captured Soviet spacecraft, Bird 1, hijack a US satellite, and thus foment nuclear war between East and West. A rapid, all-out assault on the crater was essential, and Bond called on the help of Tiger Tanaka and his Ninja fighting force.

TELL-TALE CHOPPER
Bond and Kissy realized they were on the right track when they saw a helicopter disappear through a camouflaged door into the crater.

Hydraulic door

Ninjas swarm down ropes

Map tracked courses of US satellite and Blofeld's rocket

Rubber cups clung to rock walls

SUCTION CUPS
Before the force arrived, Bond climbed down inside the crater using suction cups strapped to his hands and knees.

ABOUT TO ATTACK
Agent Kissy Suzuki prepared for the assault on the crater with her boss, Tiger Tanaka, dressed in Ninja gear.

Blofeld's monorail

ROCKET-FIRING CIGARETTE

Flame ignites fuse

Missile

HEALTH HAZARD
Blofeld permitted 007 to have a last smoke and quickly regretted it; the cigarette fired a small rocket that caused chaos in the control room.

Ninja with samurai sword

Cans of rocket fuel

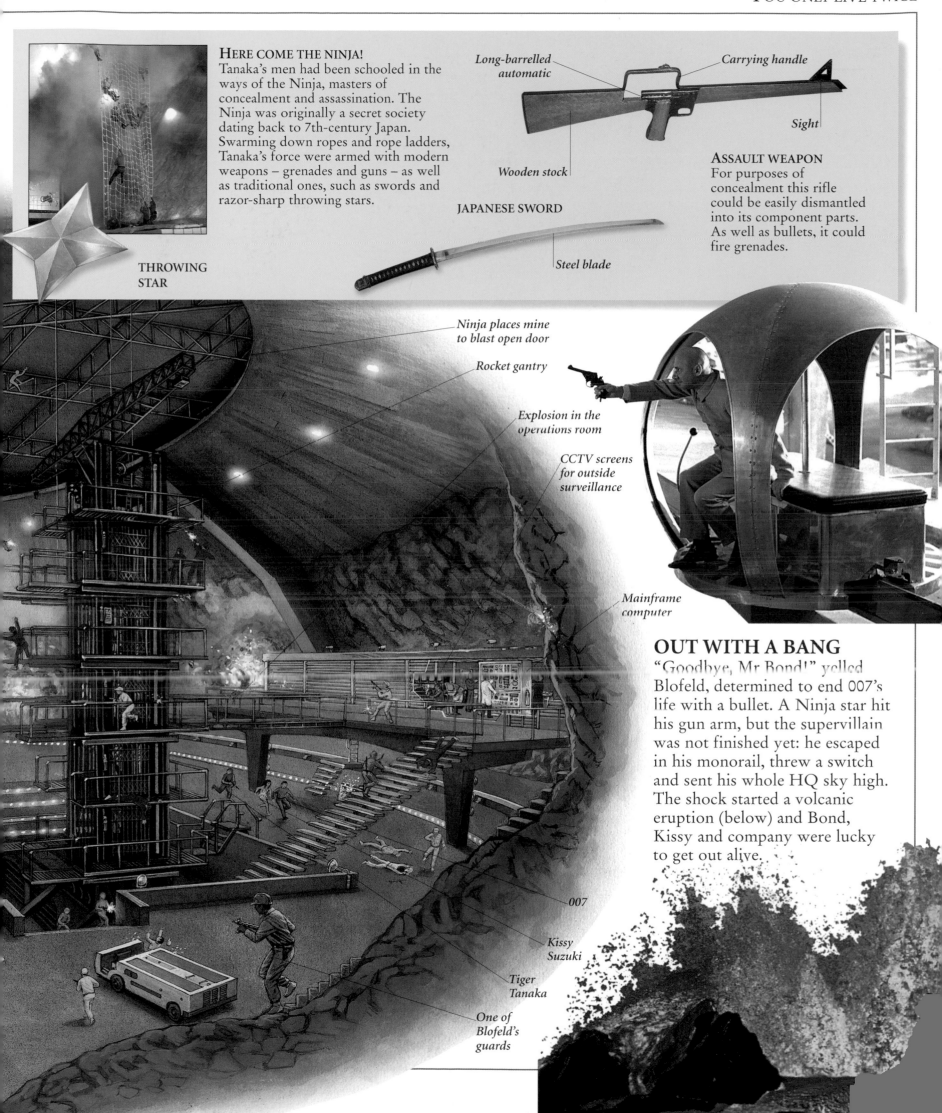

HERE COME THE NINJA!

Tanaka's men had been schooled in the ways of the Ninja, masters of concealment and assassination. The Ninja was originally a secret society dating back to 7th-century Japan. Swarming down ropes and rope ladders, Tanaka's force were armed with modern weapons – grenades and guns – as well as traditional ones, such as swords and razor-sharp throwing stars.

THROWING STAR

Long-barrelled automatic

Carrying handle

Sight

Wooden stock

Sight

ASSAULT WEAPON

For purposes of concealment this rifle could be easily dismantled into its component parts. As well as bullets, it could fire grenades.

JAPANESE SWORD

Steel blade

Ninja places mine to blast open door

Rocket gantry

Explosion in the operations room

CCTV screens for outside surveillance

Mainframe computer

OUT WITH A BANG

"Goodbye, Mr Bond!" yelled Blofeld, determined to end 007's life with a bullet. A Ninja star hit his gun arm, but the supervillain was not finished yet: he escaped in his monorail, threw a switch and sent his whole HQ sky high. The shock started a volcanic eruption (below) and Bond, Kissy and company were lucky to get out alive.

007

Kissy Suzuki

Tiger Tanaka

One of Blofeld's guards

OHMSS

RUNAWAY GIRL

After rescuing Tracy from drowning, Bond was attacked by thugs employed by her father. By the time he had fought them off she was running towards her car. But Bond sensed that they would meet again.

SPY CAMERA

Shutter release · Shutter speed dial · Focusing dial · Film speed dial · Lens · Light meter

For photographing secret documents, Bond used a standard-issue Minox miniature camera. It was just 79 mm (3.1 in) long.

A WOMAN WANDERING fully clothed into the sea – it could only mean one thing, a suicide attempt. James Bond skidded to a halt in his Aston Martin DBS and carried her from the waves. Her name was Teresa ("Tracy") di Vicenzo, and she was the beautiful, reckless daughter of crime baron Marc Ange Draco. Draco was looking for a husband to tame his wayward child and thought that Bond fitted the bill. Bond was not so sure, but Draco had a powerful bargaining tool: information on the whereabouts of Ernst Stavro Blofeld.

Barrel and trigger concealed in stock

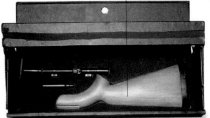

Telescopic sight

SNIPER'S RIFLE

Bond used the telescopic sight from a sniper's rifle he kept in the glove compartment of his car to spot Tracy on the beach. The rifle was his new Aston Martin's only special feature.

TRACY

Bond's next good deed was to bail Tracy out when she lost heavily at the casino. "Why do you persist in rescuing me, Mr Bond?" she asked.

Magnetic sensor

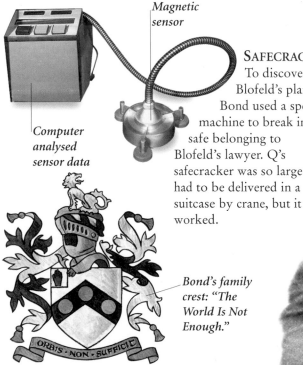

Computer analysed sensor data

SAFECRACKER

To discover Blofeld's plans, Bond used a special machine to break into a safe belonging to Blofeld's lawyer. Q's safecracker was so large it had to be delivered in a suitcase by crane, but it worked.

Bond's family crest: "The World Is Not Enough."

ORBIS · NON · SUFFICIT

MARC ANGE DRACO

Tracy's father was Marc Ange Draco, boss of the Union Corse crime syndicate. He wanted to see her settled, married to a man like Bond – "What she needs is a man to dominate her!" – and offered Bond a lead on Blofeld.

THE BOND FAMILY CREST

Draco told Bond that Blofeld was after a title. Bond made enquiries at the College of Arms in London – and discovered his own family's motto and coat of arms.

THE IMPORTANCE OF BEING ERNST

Ernst Stavro Blofeld now craved titled respectability and a pardon for past misdeeds. As always, he was prepared to stop at nothing to get his way. He had resorted to plastic surgery to alter his appearance and remove his earlobes – an hereditary characteristic of the ancient Bleuchamp family.

KILLER'S CREST

Blofeld laid claim to the title of Count de Bleuchamp. The family motto translated as "Of the air and soaring".

WINTER SPORT

In the Swiss Alps, Blofeld had set up an exclusive sanitorium, accessible only by cable car and helicopter. Bond, disguised as genealogist Sir Hilary Bray, decided to pay him a visit.

FALLING IN LOVE

His cover blown, Bond had to escape Piz Gloria in a hurry. When Tracy showed up in her Ford Cougar, the villains didn't stand a chance. Shortly afterwards, in a hayloft, Bond proposed.

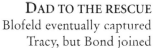

DAD TO THE RESCUE

Blofeld eventually captured Tracy, but Bond joined forces with Draco and his private army to rescue her and destroy Blofeld's mountain lair.

OUT FOR REVENGE

Enraged at seeing his carefully laid plans ruined by Bond, and humiliated when Tracy disdained his advances, Blofeld was consumed by thoughts of revenge. When he heard the couple planned to wed he resolved to make it a day to remember.

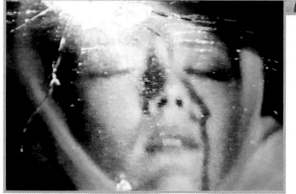

DRIVE-BY KILLING

Blofeld struck just a few hours after the wedding. A burst of machine-gun fire, and Tracy fell back in her car seat, dead. Bond's dreams of a simpler, better life died with her. Just the memory of her remained. "We have all the time in the world," he murmured.

PIZ GLORIA

HIGH UP IN THE SWISS ALPS, accessible only by cable car and helicopter, lay Piz Gloria. On the surface, Blofeld's lair was an allergy clinic. Yet, curiously, all the patients were beautiful women. Bond stumbled on the truth – they were being brainwashed into carrying deadly viruses, manufactured in Piz Gloria's secret labs.

GUARDED SECRETS

Bond, disguised as Sir Hilary Bray, a genealogist from the Royal College of Arms, asked why the sanitorium was so heavily guarded. Irma Bunt, Blofeld's second-in-command, told him the reason was the threat of industrial espionage.

Sanitorium offered spectacular mountain views

Clients socialized in the luxurious lounge

One of many deluxe rooms reserved for Dr Blofeld's clients

Revolving dining room

Modern art (stolen)

Main reception area

Cable-car wheelhouse – one of Piz Gloria's few vulnerable points

Lifts to all floors

Ladder leading to escape tunnel

Blofeld's private escape tunnel led from lift to cable-car tower

Blofeld's secret escape hatch

BLOFELD MAKES HIS MOVE
Captured following an avalanche, Tracy played for time by pretending to tolerate Blofeld's slimy advances. Fortunately she did not have to wait too long before 007, and Marc Ange Draco, her crime-boss father, came to the rescue.

ANGELS OF DEATH
Blofeld had discovered a virus that induced sterility in animals and plants. He planned to spread the virus – and decimate world food stocks – using his "angels of death", a group of girls from various countries whom he had brainwashed. The poor things had only checked in for an allergy cure!

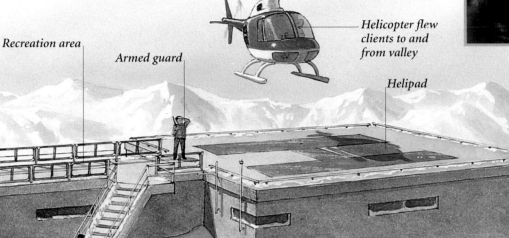

Recreation area

Armed guard

Helicopter flew clients to and from valley

Helipad

Virus contained in atomiser

Antenna

Receiver

On/off switch

DEADLY COMPACT
Each patient was presented with a gift pack containing a receiver disguised as a compact – to pick up Blofeld's orders – and an atomiser containing the virus.

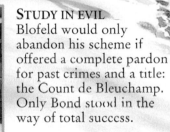

STUDY IN EVIL
Blofeld would only abandon his scheme if offered a complete pardon for past crimes and a title: the Count de Bleuchamp. Only Bond stood in the way of total success.

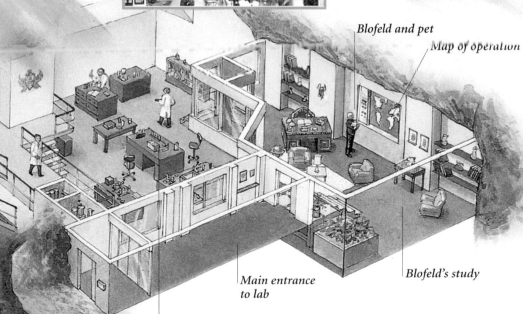

Blofeld and pet

Map of operation

Blofeld's study

Main entrance to lab

Research laboratory

LABORATORY
The nerve-centre of Piz Gloria, the laboratories were where Blofeld's deadly bacteria were developed. Bond knew that the world would not be safe until they were utterly destroyed – and preferably Blofeld with them.

ATTACK FORCE
Bond's final assault on Piz Gloria was aided by men from Draco's crime empire, who soon put the bite on Blofeld's orange-clad guards.

DIAMONDS ARE FOREVER

LOCAL KNOWLEDGE
A girl called Marie gave Bond Blofeld's location – after a little persuasion.

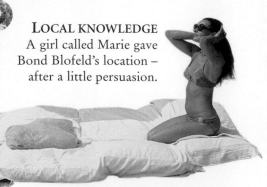

RESOLVED TO AVENGE Tracy's murder, Bond tracked Blofeld to Egypt and watched him die in a mud pool. Back in London, M assigned 007 to infiltrate a smuggling ring and find out who was stockpiling stolen diamonds. Impersonating a gang-member named Franks, Bond contacted another, Tiffany Case, and travelled to Las Vegas with a hoard of gems hidden in Franks' coffin. The diamonds were required by a hi-tech empire belonging to a reclusive tycoon. But lurking in the background, back from the dead, was Bond's most bitter foe – and this time there were two of him!

MUDDY WATER
Bond was sure Blofeld's murderous career was over. How could anyone have survived this boiling mud bath?

SIN CITY
A town founded on greed – what better place for a jewel-smuggling racket than Las Vegas?

ASHES TO ASHES
An urn, supposedly for Franks' ashes, was used to conceal the smuggled diamonds.

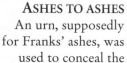

TIFFANY CASE
Used to living by her wits, jewel smuggler Tiffany thought she'd seen it all – until she met James Bond. She tried to wear him like a diamond ring, but he had more facets than she realized.

DESERT RATS
Bond pursued his enquiries amid a spate of murders, including that of a dentist who worked for a South African diamond mine. He was killed in the desert by Wint and Kidd, who dropped a scorpion down his back. It emerged that he had been smuggling uncut gems from the mine.

WILLARD WHYTE
Multi-millionaire recluse Whyte owned the massive conglomerate W. Techtronics. Held prisoner in his mansion, he was unaware that his company was being misused by Ernst Stavro Blofeld.

THUMP, THUMP
Bond made a crucial breakthrough in the case when he managed to free Willard Whyte from imprisonment in his own house. To do so, 007 had to subdue two gymnastic female guards, Bambi and Thumper.

DUNE ROAMING
Bond infiltrated Whyte's factory in the Nevada desert. When guards spotted him, he escaped in one of the company's latest inventions, a Moonbuggy.

"Hi, I'm Plenty."
"But of course you are,"
replied Bond

PLENTY OF NOTHING
Happy-go-lucky casino girl Plenty O'Toole was attracted to Bond, and so became a tragic victim. She was found dead in a swimming pool, possibly killed in mistake for Tiffany Case.

BERT SAXBY
Whyte's treacherous right-hand man, Saxby cleared the way for Blofeld to use Whyte's "nice little company" for his own evil ends.

WINT & KIDD
Blofeld employed these two assassins to cover his tracks by rubbing out everyone involved in the diamond smuggling racket. A deadly, sadistic pair, they really loved their work.

DR METZ
This brilliant scientist deluded himself that Blofeld was mankind's benefactor and a believer in world disarmament.

W TECTRONICS

NAME
METZ
POSITION
SPECIAL
ISSUED
7-5-71
SIGNATURE
K. Metz

SX 8352DI

Diamond necklace

ERNST STAVRO BLOFELD
Having created doubles of himself to confuse Bond, and with enough diamonds to arm a superweapon to bring the West to its knees, Blofeld believed himself invulnerable.

OIL RIG BATTLE

THANKS TO BOND'S detective work, US military might was at last closing in on Blofeld's oil-rig lair, the control centre for his orbiting satellite superweapon. "This farcical show was only to be expected," Blofeld scoffed, "– the great powers flexing their muscles like so many impotent beach boys." But while he activated the rig's defences and prepared his own escape, he forgot that the "great powers" had a special agent on board – James Bond.

SATELLITE DEATH RAY
Out in space circled Blofeld's diamond-encrusted superweapon – its laser beam capable of reducing any target on Earth to ashes.

THE PEACENIK
Blofeld had conned his top personnel into thinking that his aim was world disarmament. He convinced them by using his superweapon to destroy US and Russian missile sites. His agenda was, of course, quite different – to hold the world to ransom.

Hatch for one-person cockpit

Headlight aids underwater visibility

Fibreglass hull

BATH-O-SUB TIME
"Prepare my Bath-o-sub," cried Blofeld realizing the battle was lost. Bond commandeered the launch crane and used the sub (with Blofeld in it) like a wrecking ball to smash the rig's control room and disable the satellite superweapon.

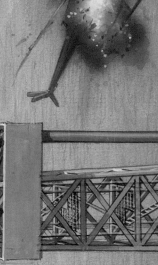

UH-1H HUEY
attack helicopter

M60
machine gun

▼ **2.**

THE HIGH WIRE
Bond escaped from his cell through a hatch and scrambled along a wire running beneath the rig.

▲ **3.**

GOING OVERBOARD
While Bond worked the crane carrying the bath-o-sub, Tiffany tried to hold off Blofeld's guards. The machine-gun's recoil was more powerful than she expected.

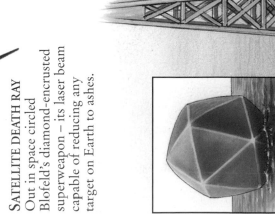

▲ **1.** *WAVE WALKER*
A plane dropped a capsule with Bond inside into the sea. Bond walked towards the rig. He unzipped the capsule's plastic skin, came aboard – and was placed under guard.

Helipad

Covered radar dish

Metal sections drop down to reveal gun

20 mm cannon

007 at the controls

Crane driver (knocked out)

Blofeld in Bath-o-sub

Westroleum

16037

MARINES

LOACH light observation helicopter

Air-to-surface missile hits gun emplacement

Blofeld's office

Control centre smashed by swinging Bath-o-sub

Satellite communications centre equipment short-circuiting

Bath-o-sub cradle

LIVE AND LET DIE

SAN MONIQUE
The island's crest celebrated
its unspoilt, Caribbean allure.

THREE MI6 AGENTS HAD DIED: in New Orleans, on the island of San Monique, and in Harlem, New York. M dispatched 007 to investigate. Bond's arrival in Harlem was predicted by a medium named Solitaire, and he was immediately a marked man. Her guardian, Dr Kananga, ruled the island of San Monique. Under the alias of Harlem hood Mr Big, he planned to flood the US with home-grown heroin, and relied on Solitaire's uncanny skill with a tarot pack to keep several steps ahead of the law.

CHAMPION OF HIS PEOPLE
Dr Kananga presented himself to the world at large as a progressive humanitarian championing the rights of his people at the United Nations. The reality was very different.

SOLITAIRE
Utterly dominated by Kananga since childhood, Solitaire was an innocent in the ways of the world. Kananga knew that her virginal state gave her second sight. Yet she had had enough of being his puppet and longed for a life of her own. She sought help in the cards: what would the future bring?

Was Bond the joker in Solitaire's pack?

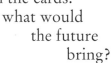

THE FOOL

THE LOVERS
Bond convinced Solitaire to fall in love with him by preparing a special pack for her – every card was the same. Soon, Solitaire's powers of prediction were on the wane.

VI

THE LOVERS

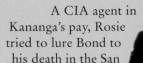

BARON SAMEDI
This enigmatic, sinister voodoo shaman ensured that the people of San Monique tended Kananga's poppy fields and did what they were told. He took his name from the all-knowing voodoo god of death.

Baron Samedi's flute was also a walkie-talkie

DR KANANGA
Affecting an air of urbanity and sophistication, Kananga was a merciless dictator. Yet his insecurities led him to try to humiliate 007 – a fatal error.

ROSIE CARVER
A CIA agent in Kananga's pay, Rosie tried to lure Bond to his death in the San Monique jungle. When she failed, Kananga's armed surveillance system – disguised as spooky scarecrows – shot her down.

Fortunately 007 was not taken in by Rosie's looks

CROCODILE FARM
The raw opium from Kananga's San Monique poppy fields was refined into heroin at a crocodile farm he owned outside New Orleans, Louisiana.

TRESPASSERS WILL BE EATEN

A sign gave fair warning to intruders

Claw powerful enough to twist gun barrels

STEEL CLAW
Bond later threw Tee Hee from a train, but his arm remained behind. Bond presented it to Q-Branch as a souvenir.

Shoulder piece

TEE HEE
Despite his name, Bond found nothing humorous about this giant enforcer. A brush with a crocodile had lead to the loss of an arm, but had in no way diminished Tee Hee's strength. He particularly relished cornering Bond on Kananga's crocodile farm in Louisiana.

ON THE BAYOU
Bond's investigations into Kananga's drug empire led him to fall foul of the Louisiana police. They soon found out that chasing 007 was one thing, catching him quite another.

KANANGA'S HIDEAWAY

Timer

Mine

THE LAIR OF DRUG BARON Dr Kananga was an underground cavern. Its entrance lay in a graveyard, where voodoo priests practised their evil magic. That night the terrorized folk of San Monique gathered to witness a human sacrifice. A woman was to be the victim – Solitaire. Now that her soothsaying powers had waned, Kananga had decided to show what happened to those that failed him. Bond waited in the shadows as the drums reached a crescendo. He had a few surprises in store for the voodoo priests and their puffed-up leader ...

MINED AREA
While the watchers were gripped by the antics of a voodoo priest in a goat mask, Bond placed two mines nearby to cause a diversion.

1. MOMENT OF TERROR ▶
Solitaire screamed as a priest in a goat mask selected a poisonous snake from a coffin full of the reptiles and waved it in her face. Then a more powerful priest, Baron Samedi, appeared.

007 frees Solitaire

▼ **2. PANIC SPREADS**
007 shot the goat-man, threw Baron Samedi into the snake-filled coffin, and cut Solitaire free. His mines then exploded, causing widespread panic.

Baron Samedi falls into coffin

Bond attacks Baron Samedi

007 shoots goat priest

Entrance to Kananga's cave beneath gravestone

◀ **3. INTO THE LAIR**
Bond and Solitaire descended underground in a lift concealed beneath a gravestone. They leapt out at Kananga's guards, catching them by surprise.

4. PASSAGE TO FEAR ▲
The couple got past the guards, passed through a steel door and entered a huge cavern.

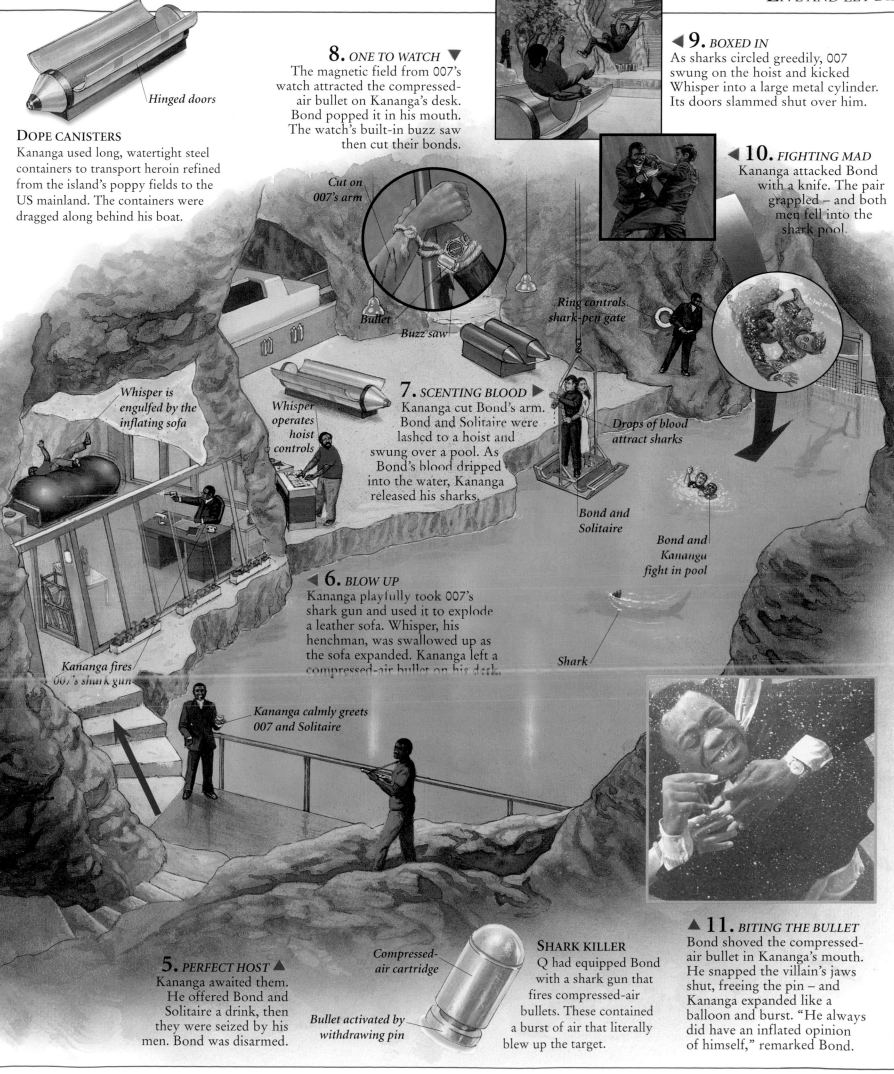

DOPE CANISTERS
Kananga used long, watertight steel containers to transport heroin refined from the island's poppy fields to the US mainland. The containers were dragged along behind his boat.

Hinged doors

8. ONE TO WATCH ▼
The magnetic field from 007's watch attracted the compressed-air bullet on Kananga's desk. Bond popped it in his mouth. The watch's built-in buzz saw then cut their bonds.

Cut on 007's arm

Bullet

Buzz saw

9. BOXED IN
As sharks circled greedily, 007 swung on the hoist and kicked Whisper into a large metal cylinder. Its doors slammed shut over him.

10. FIGHTING MAD
Kananga attacked Bond with a knife. The pair grappled – and both men fell into the shark pool.

Whisper is engulfed by the inflating sofa

Whisper operates hoist controls

Ring controls shark-pen gate

7. SCENTING BLOOD ▶
Kananga cut Bond's arm. Bond and Solitaire were lashed to a hoist and swung over a pool. As Bond's blood dripped into the water, Kananga released his sharks.

Drops of blood attract sharks

Bond and Solitaire

Bond and Kananga fight in pool

◀ 6. BLOW UP
Kananga playfully took 007's shark gun and used it to explode a leather sofa. Whisper, his henchman, was swallowed up as the sofa expanded. Kananga left a compressed-air bullet on his desk.

Shark

Kananga fires 007's shark gun

Kananga calmly greets 007 and Solitaire

5. PERFECT HOST ▲
Kananga awaited them. He offered Bond and Solitaire a drink, then they were seized by his men. Bond was disarmed.

Compressed-air cartridge

Bullet activated by withdrawing pin

SHARK KILLER
Q had equipped Bond with a shark gun that fires compressed-air bullets. These contained a burst of air that literally blew up the target.

▲ 11. BITING THE BULLET
Bond shoved the compressed-air bullet in Kananga's mouth. He snapped the villain's jaws shut, freeing the pin – and Kananga expanded like a balloon and burst. "He always did have an inflated opinion of himself," remarked Bond.

THE MAN WITH THE GOLDEN GUN

A GOLD BULLET ARRIVED at MI6 with "007" inscribed on it. Only one man was known to favour gold bullets: Scaramanga, the world's deadliest assassin. Bond set aside his current assignment – searching for a missing solar-energy scientist called Gibson – to get Scaramanga before Scaramanga got him. A bullet in a belly dancer's navel supplied one clue and Scaramanga's girlfriend Andrea provided another. However Bond soon realized that he was not Scaramanga's prime target after all. Scaramanga was more interested in obtaining the Solex Agitator, a device that could convert the sun's radiation into a deadly weapon. And he would kill anyone in his way.

ANDREA
Scaramanga's girlfriend Andrea Anders was sick of his sadistic games. It was she who sent the gold bullet to MI6 that set Bond on Scaramanga's tail. She later paid the ultimate price for turning against her brutal lover.

GUN MAKER
MI6 traced the bullet to a shady Macau gunsmith called Lazar. Bond made him reveal that Scaramanga's next consignment of bullets was soon to be collected by Andrea Anders.

UNDER SURVEILLANCE
Bond followed Andrea on a hydrofoil to Hong Kong's Peninsula Hotel. He was confident she would lead him straight to Scaramanga.

MARY GOODNIGHT
MI6 agent Mary spent a night in a cupboard just to keep in close contact with 007. M later dismissed rumours of a romance.

Pen formed barrel

Lighter formed bullet chamber

Bullet was 23-carat gold with traces of nickel

THE GOLDEN GUN
Scaramanga's trademark weapon was a single-shot, gold-plated, 4.2-calibre handgun. Amazingly, it could be assembled from a few everyday objects: a cigarette case, a lighter, a cuff link and a pen.

Cufflink formed trigger

Cigarette case formed butt

STREET SHOOTING
Instead of finding Scaramanga, Bond witnessed his handiwork – the murder of the solar-energy scientist Gibson outside a sleazy nightclub. A strange little man lurked near the crime scene, but the police arrested Bond.

NICK NACK
Scaramanga's pint-sized henchman annoyed 007 right up until the very end of the mission.

HAI FAT
This Hong Kong magnate employed Scaramanga to kill the scientist Gibson and seize the Solex Agitator. He was later calmly murdered by Scaramanga, his so-called "junior partner".

CHULA
The martial arts supremo at Hai Fat's kung-fu school was pitted against 007, who used rather less sophisticated techniques to defeat him.

OVER THE TOP
While chasing Scaramanga, Bond pulled off an amazing manoeuvre. He accelerated up a broken-down jetty and flew across a canal to land upright on the opposite bank. The car's trajectory was captured in this photograph from MI6 files.

SHERIFF J. W. PEPPER
The police chief led a dance by 007 during the *Live and Let Die* mission was holidaying with his wife in Bangkok when he became mixed up in Bond's pursuit of Scaramanga.

FLY-DRIVE BREAK
Cornered by Bond in a shed, Scaramanga made a flying getaway. His AMC Matador car suddenly sprouted wings and jetted off into the blue.

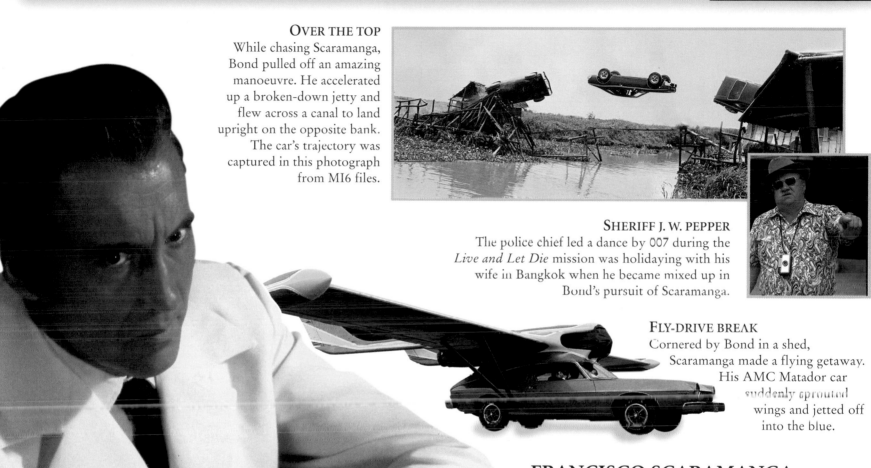

FRANCISCO SCARAMANGA
The assassin prided himself on only ever needing one bullet to finish a job. No photographs of him existed; all MI6 knew of his appearance was that he had a third nipple – a sign of invulnerability. A man of taste, he was a lone wolf similar in some ways to 007, but with a streak of merciless cruelty. He admired Bond and even kept a mannequin of him at his island retreat. Bond had nothing but contempt for the man and his methods.

HOUSE OF FUN

Scaramanga's island hideaway was equipped with every modern electrical convenience – all powered by solar energy. He also possessed a solar gun that could fire a devastating beam. However his mansion's most amazing feature was the "Funhouse", a lethal labyrinth of mirrors and murderous mannequins. It was here, in cat and mouse duels orchestrated by Nick Nack, Scaramanga's henchman, that the master assassin honed his skills. When he challenged Bond to single combat "between titans", 007 was duty-bound to accept.

SUN BURNT
To demonstrate his solar gun, Scaramanga incinerated the seaplane that had brought 007 to the island.

THE SOLEX AGITATOR
This small device transmitted solar energy to thermal generators, creating vast reserves of power that could be used for peaceful or destructive purposes.

Solar gun

LUNCH WITH A KILLER
Bond and Mary Goodnight were entertained to a *cordon bleu* feast prepared by Nick Nack. The food was excellent, but Scaramanga's post-prandial challenge of a duel to the death was less easy on Bond's stomach. 007 elected to finish his lunch first.

Controls for solar panels

Panel directed sun's rays down to thermal generators

POWER SOURCE
Solar panels that rose up from off-shore rocky outcrops provided the power source for Scaramanga's lair.

Solar panel

▼ **1.** *BACK TO BACK*
Down on the sunlit beach, Bond and Scaramanga stood back to back to begin the duel. Nick Nack started a count of 20.

007's Walther PPK held six shots

Scaramanga's golden gun had one shot

▲ **2.** *FIRST SHOT*
The count ended and 007 turned and fired. But Scaramanga had vanished - and now 007 had one less bullet.

▲ **3.** *DOOR TO DEATH*
Nick Nack directed Bond to the door of the Funhouse, where Scaramanga awaited him.

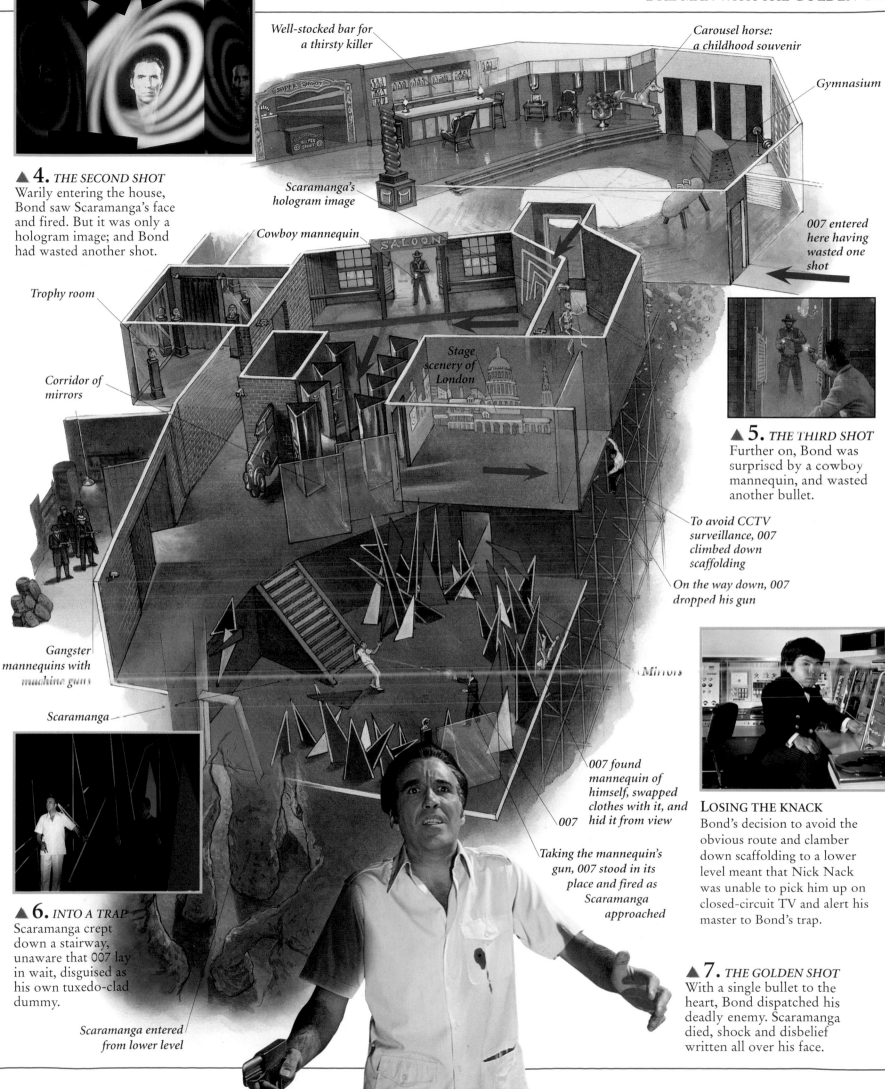

▲ **4.** *THE SECOND SHOT*
Warily entering the house, Bond saw Scaramanga's face and fired. But it was only a hologram image; and Bond had wasted another shot.

Well-stocked bar for a thirsty killer

Carousel horse: a childhood souvenir

Gymnasium

Scaramanga's hologram image

007 entered here having wasted one shot

Cowboy mannequin

Trophy room

Corridor of mirrors

SALOON

Stage scenery of London

▲ **5.** *THE THIRD SHOT*
Further on, Bond was surprised by a cowboy mannequin, and wasted another bullet.

To avoid CCTV surveillance, 007 climbed down scaffolding

On the way down, 007 dropped his gun

Gangster mannequins with machine guns

Mirrors

007 found mannequin of himself, swapped clothes with it, and hid it from view

007

Scaramanga

LOSING THE KNACK
Bond's decision to avoid the obvious route and clamber down scaffolding to a lower level meant that Nick Nack was unable to pick him up on closed-circuit TV and alert his master to Bond's trap.

Taking the mannequin's gun, 007 stood in its place and fired as Scaramanga approached

▲ **6.** *INTO A TRAP*
Scaramanga crept down a stairway, unaware that 007 lay in wait, disguised as his own tuxedo-clad dummy.

Scaramanga entered from lower level

▲ **7.** *THE GOLDEN SHOT*
With a single bullet to the heart, Bond dispatched his deadly enemy. Scaramanga died, shock and disbelief written all over his face.

THE SPY WHO LOVED ME

TWO ATOMIC SUBMARINES belonging to the British and Soviet navies had vanished. MI6 and the KGB assigned their best agents to the case, and so James Bond, 007, found himself working with Major Anya Amasova, Agent Triple-X. Bond and Anya learned that plans for a new submarine tracking system were on sale to the highest bidder. Suspecting a link with the missing subs, they resolved to get hold of the plans. However they faced awesome competition from a monstrous killing machine called Jaws and his boss, Karl Stromberg.

FATAL BULLET
On assignment in Siberia, 007 shot a KGB assassin using a ski-pole gun. The victim was the lover of 007's next partner, Anya Amasova.

CLOSING IN
The mystery of the missing subs was solved when MI6 obtained a picture of the bows of shipping magnate Karl Stromberg's supertanker the *Liparus*, opening like jaws to engulf HMS *Ranger*, a Royal Navy submarine.

ANYA AMASOVA
She won 007 over by getting hold of the microfilm of the submarine tracking system. Bond then spotted that the plans bore Stromberg's crest. Bond didn't know that Anya had vowed to kill him after the mission for shooting her KGB boyfriend.

Insignia of Stromberg's shipping line

NUCLEAR CARGO
Stromberg's growing collection of nuclear submarines was housed in the vast interior of the *Liparus*. He had not captured them to indulge in a little underwater exploration. He was more interested in the arsenals of nuclear missiles they carried.

LUXURY LIVING
Buying the plans for the submarine tracking system took Bond and Anya to Cairo, and a rendezvous at a top nightclub. Unfortunately their contact ended up dead.

SUCCESSFUL MISSION
After locating a sub using a special tracking system, the *Liparus* captured the unsuspecting craft. The *Liparus'* captain then radioed Stromberg with the good news.

SECRET BASE
Q had accompanied 007 to Cairo, establishing a base in a pyramid. He demonstrated some of his latest inventions, including a deadly, spring-loaded pouffe.

STROMBERG

Secure in his off-shore lair, *Atlantis*, Stromberg enjoyed soothing classical music (Bach, Mozart), plotting to decimate the human race, and taking revenge on anyone he suspected of swindling him.

NAOMI

"What a handsome craft," Bond remarked on meeting Naomi, Stromberg's pilot. He was less impressed when she took to the skies in her helicopter and tried to gun him and Anya down.

JAWS

Urged by Stromberg to "eliminate" anyone connected with the missing microfilm of the submarine tracking system, Jaws took his work seriously. The 7-ft giant with razor-sharp metal teeth left a trail of destruction and dead bodies in his wake.

BATTLE ON BOARD

Despite being held prisoner on the *Liparus*, Bond, Anya and the crew of the submarine USS *Wayne* managed to attack Stromberg's forces and destroy his sea-going base from

BIG BANGER

Bond used an atomic detonator to blast into the *Liparus*'s control room and foil Stromberg's plan to blow up New York and Moscow with nuclear missiles.

ANYA KIDNAPPED

Amid the chaos of battle aboard the *Liparus*, Stromberg and his men took Anya hostage and fled to *Atlantis*.

Microfilm of sub tracking system

WET NELLIE

SIDECAR SUICIDE
Attacked by a motorcyclist with a sidecar bomb, the wide-tyred Lotus Esprit displayed its superb handling. The sidecar missed, hitting a lorry, and the rider went over a cliff.

Rocket-powered sidecar bomb

Telescopic periscope gave 360° field of vision

AIR DEFENCE
To protect against aircraft attack, the Lotus possessed radar-guided surface-to-air missiles, which fired upward from an emplacement in the rear hatch.

FOR *THE SPY WHO LOVED ME* mission, Q supplied 007 with a Lotus Esprit – one of the most remarkable vehicles ever entrusted to Bond's tender care. In addition to various "standard-issue" weapons, at the flick of a switch the wheels withdrew and the car converted into a submarine. Nicknamed "Wet Nellie" by MI6, the Lotus was ideal for an undersea reconnaissance of Stromberg's off-shore laboratory, Atlantis.

TAKING THE PLUNGE
Pursued by a helicopter firing machine guns, Bond drove off a jetty straight into the Mediterranean. In a matter of moments, the car became a submarine – and the hunted became the hunter…

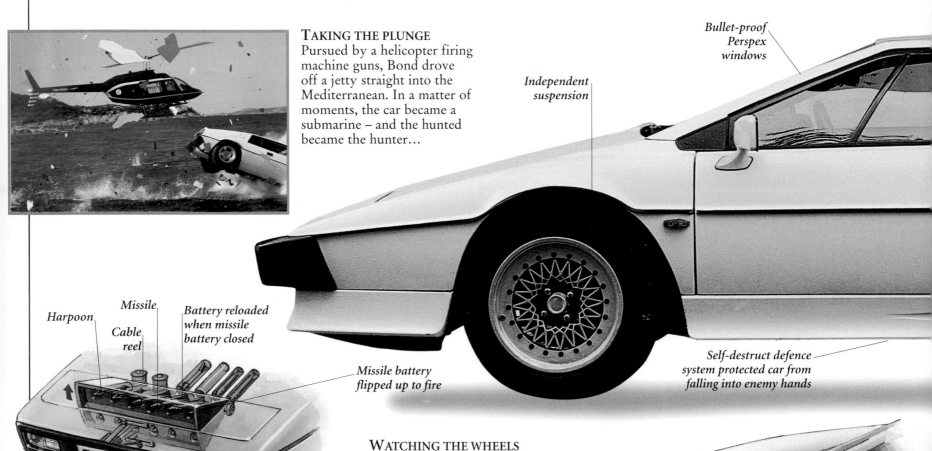

Bullet-proof Perspex windows

Independent suspension

Self-destruct defence system protected car from falling into enemy hands

Harpoon

Missile

Cable reel

Battery reloaded when missile battery closed

Missile battery flipped up to fire

PPW 306R

POWER-PACKED
The Lotus's elegant bonnet housed a battery of four undersea, heat-seeking missile launchers. Missiles could be fired individually or together. The middle two contained stun grenades; the right-hand two, explosive warheads. Two harpoons attached to 50 metres (164 ft) of cable completed the battery.

WATCHING THE WHEELS
For submarine mode, the front-wheel retractor mechanism disconnected the steering, and the rear-wheel mechanism disconnected the engine transmission. The front and rear wheels swung upwards through 90° and withdrew into the body.

Wheel-arch doors fully locked

Hydroplane activator slid hydroplanes through wheel-arch doors when wheels were fully withdrawn and wheel-arch doors had locked

Hydroplane

Wheel swung upwards

Wheel retractor mechanism

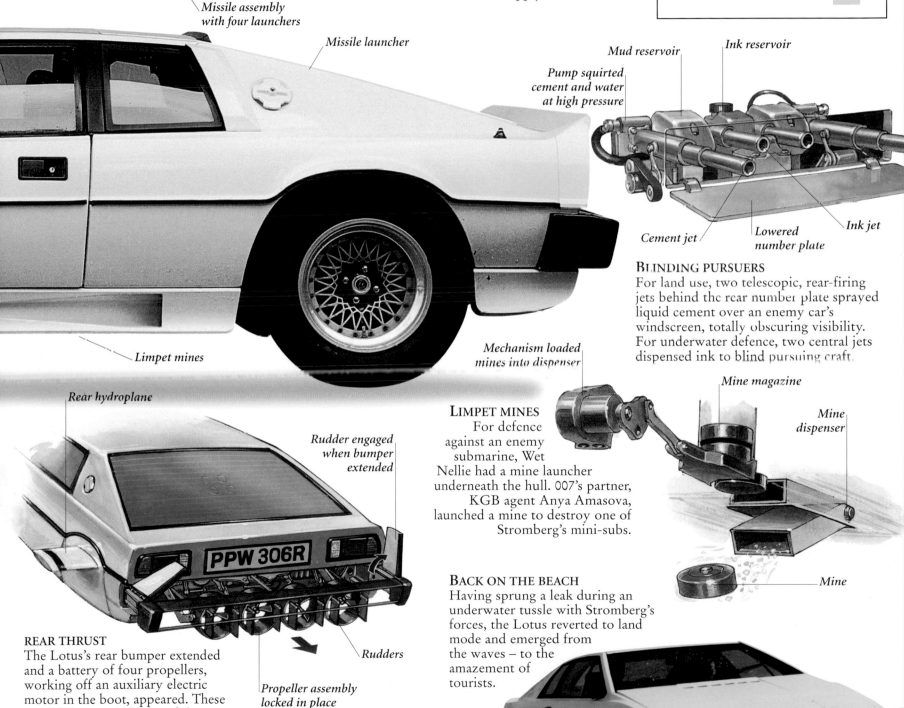

Circular valves allow missiles to be fired underwater

Missile assembly with four launchers

DIVING DOWN
Wet Nellie's body was a single, glass-fibre shell, lightweight, durable, and most important, watertight. The craft could dive to a depth of 100 metres (328 ft). Its tanks had two hours' supply of air.

LOTUS ESPRIT: SPECIFICATIONS
- **Max. speed:** 138 mph (221 km/h)
- **Acceleration:** 0–60 mph (0–96 km/h) in 6.8 seconds)
- **Engine** 2-litre, 16-valve, four cylinder
- **Length:** 419.1cm (13 ft 9 in)
- **Width:** 185 cm (6 ft 1 in)
- **Engine capacity:** 1,973 cc

Missile launcher

Mud reservoir

Ink reservoir

Pump squirted cement and water at high pressure

Cement jet

Lowered number plate

Ink jet

Limpet mines

BLINDING PURSUERS
For land use, two telescopic, rear-firing jets behind the rear number plate sprayed liquid cement over an enemy car's windscreen, totally obscuring visibility. For underwater defence, two central jets dispensed ink to blind pursuing craft.

Mechanism loaded mines into dispenser

Mine magazine

Mine dispenser

Rear hydroplane

Rudder engaged when bumper extended

LIMPET MINES
For defence against an enemy submarine, Wet Nellie had a mine launcher underneath the hull. 007's partner, KGB agent Anya Amasova, launched a mine to destroy one of Stromberg's mini-subs.

Mine

PPW 306R

REAR THRUST
The Lotus's rear bumper extended and a battery of four propellers, working off an auxiliary electric motor in the boot, appeared. These provided up to 16 knots of thrust underwater. The sub had a range of some 48 km (30 miles).

Propeller assembly locked in place

Rudders

BACK ON THE BEACH
Having sprung a leak during an underwater tussle with Stromberg's forces, the Lotus reverted to land mode and emerged from the waves – to the amazement of tourists.

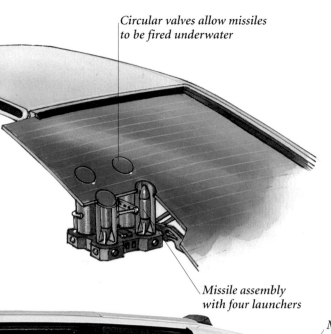

PPW 306R

ATLANTIS

STROMBERG'S sea-going lair was a massive submersible, the dream home of a billionaire recluse who despised every aspect of terrestrial civilization. Its crab-like design and impressive aquarium filled with exotic, deadly marine life reflected its owner's dark obsession with the sea and with power. For *Atlantis* also functioned as the nerve-centre of Stromberg's plan to wipe out life on land and create an underwater city with himself as sole ruler. *Atlantis* had to be destroyed.

UP FROM THE DEPTHS
Like a fairy-tale sea monster, Atlantis comes to the surface, its circular "body" supported on four giant legs.

UNDERWATER WORLD

Atlantis was the only place the paranoid, reclusive Stromberg felt at home. "For me this is all the world," he declared. "There is beauty. There is ugliness. And there is death." The hi-tech study was where he relaxed, hatched his plans for world domination, and briefed subordinates, such as Jaws, to do his murderous bidding out in the wide world.

FLOATING AROUND THE MED
Atlantis rose 200 metres (656 ft) into the air. It was supported on gigantic pontoons which rested on the sea bed while the craft was stationary. *Atlantis* had no engine, but was towed from place to place along the Mediterranean coast by Stromberg's supertanker the *Liparus*.

Main entrance area

Laboratory

Aquarium

Deadly poisonous dorsal spines

Stromberg's lionfish

SIZE MATTERS
Bond explored *Atlantis* in his Lotus submarine, and fought off Stromberg's divers. The picture above gives some idea of *Atlantis'* huge size. The Lotus is nearing the divers' access point on the craft's right "leg".

NATURAL WASTAGE
Stromberg's aquarium of sharks and other deadly fish was his pride and joy. His pets eagerly devoured any disobedient members of his staff.

PRETTY POISON
One of Stromberg's favourite specimens was his lionfish. Like its owner, it was handsome but deadly, and kept to itself.

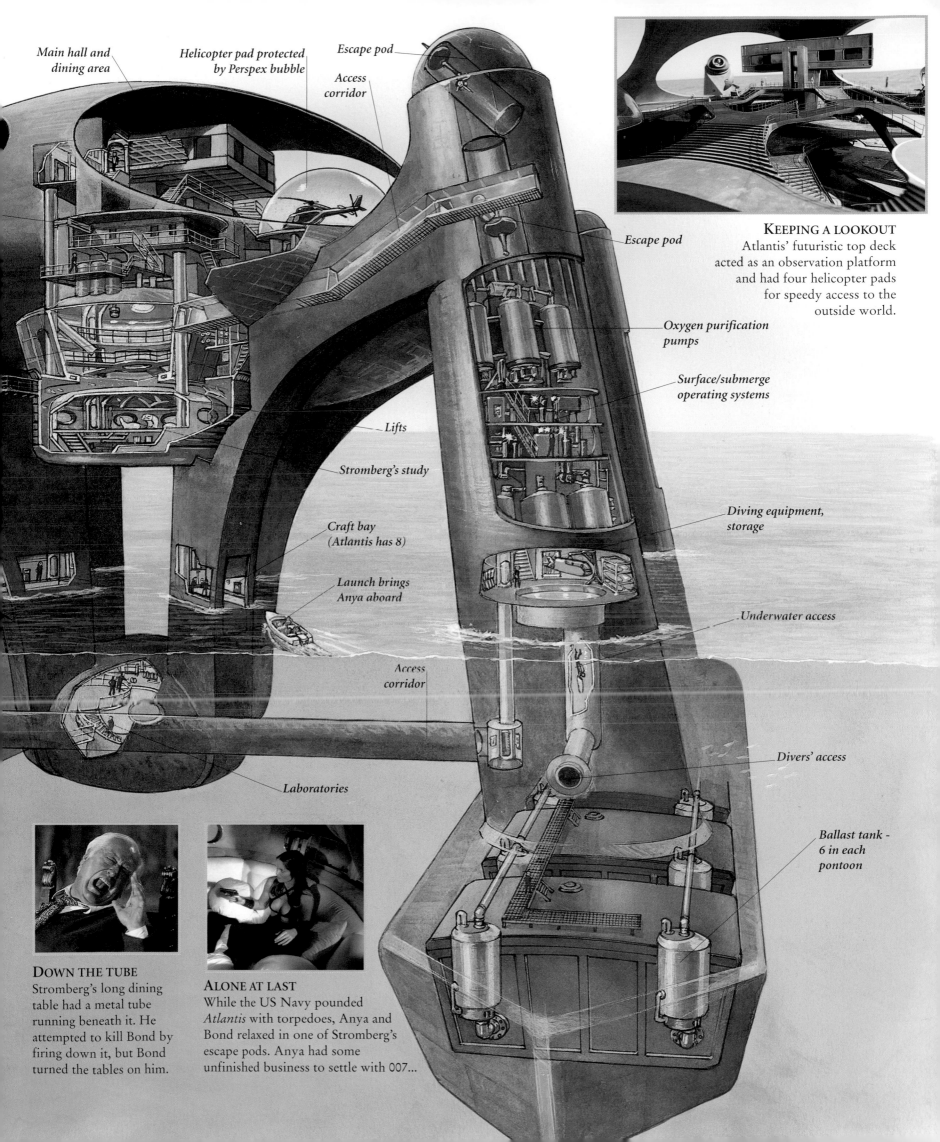

Main hall and dining area

Helicopter pad protected by Perspex bubble

Escape pod

Access corridor

Escape pod

KEEPING A LOOKOUT
Atlantis' futuristic top deck acted as an observation platform and had four helicopter pads for speedy access to the outside world.

Oxygen purification pumps

Surface/submerge operating systems

Lifts

Stromberg's study

Diving equipment, storage

Craft bay (Atlantis has 8)

Launch brings Anya aboard

Underwater access

Access corridor

Divers' access

Laboratories

Ballast tank – 6 in each pontoon

DOWN THE TUBE
Stromberg's long dining table had a metal tube running beneath it. He attempted to kill Bond by firing down it, but Bond turned the tables on him.

ALONE AT LAST
While the US Navy pounded *Atlantis* with torpedoes, Anya and Bond relaxed in one of Stromberg's escape pods. Anya had some unfinished business to settle with 007...

SKYDIVE DUEL

TROUBLE WAS IN THE AIR, but Bond didn't know it as he flew back from a successful African assignment. In a matter of moments, he found himself plummeting earthwards without a parachute. To make matters even worse, his old enemy Jaws, like some monstrous vulture, was itching to take a bite out of him. Thousands of metres up, the pair met in one of 007's most unforgettable duels.

HOSTESS SERVICE

Bond was in a relaxed mood – and so, it appeared, was the hostess in his lap. "I don't think I'm going to fly with anyone else," Bond sighed. Suddenly he was looking down the barrel of a gun. "You're so right, Mr Bond," the girl snapped. Then the pilot appeared, wearing a parachute, and Bond knew he really had problems.

▼ **1.** *LAST CHANCE*
The pilot, after shooting at the plane's controls, opened the exit door. 007 hung on as the pilot tried to push him out.

OUT FOR BLOOD
After Bond had bested him time and time again during *The Spy Who Loved Me* mission, Jaws was in no mood to let his quarry escape this time.

▼ **4.** *LIFE AND DEATH*
The pilot fell helplessly as 007 wrestled the parachute off his back and buckled it on.

▲ **3.** *MID-AIR BATTLE*
Bond skydived after the pilot, determined to snatch his parachute.

▲ **2.** *ABOVE THE CLOUDS*
With an adroit twist, Bond pushed the pilot out. Suddenly a hefty shove in the back hurled Bond into space.

BITE OF STEEL
Jaws' stainless steel teeth were as indestructible as the man himself. This set was recovered by MI6 operatives.

5. WATCH THE SKIES ▲
Bond went into freefall unaware that a dark shape was looming above him and closing fast.

6. BIRD OF PREY ▲
Jaws swooped down upon the helpless figure of Bond.

▲7. ONCE BITTEN...
The enemies grappled with each other. Clinging to Bond, Jaws bared his metal teeth to chew a chunk out of his leg.

▼8. TOO MUCH FORCE
Bond opened his parachute and the force ripped him from Jaws' grasp. Jaws yanked his rip cord, but it snapped.

▲9. SAFETY NET
While Bond floated peacefully to earth, Jaws dropped like a stone. Just in time he saw a large tent, and flapped his arms to position himself over it.

▲10. WHAT A CIRCUS!
Jaws thudded into the big top, bringing it crashing to the ground.

11. STRONG AND SILENT ▲
Jaws staggered out of the tent, unharmed. A single glance skyward spoke volumes.

MOONRAKER

A US SPACE SHUTTLE named *Moonraker* had vanished while being transported by the RAF. To solve this highly embarrassing situation for the British government, M sent 007 to California to question the man responsible for building the shuttle, Hugo Drax. Bond's suspicions about Drax deepened after he narrowly escaped death during a tour of Drax's technical facilities. He joined forces with Holly Goodhead, a scientist and CIA agent who had infiltrated Drax's space programme and, little by little, the poisonous nature of Drax's masterplan emerged.

MISSING SPACECRAFT
Moonraker could be launched by a rocket, orbit the Earth, re-enter Earth's atmosphere, and land just like a conventional aircraft.

Holly's handbag acted as a radio receiver

CORINNE DUFOUR
Bond's guide around Drax's estate, Corinne was a free spirit who was soon attracted to Bond. When she discovered him searching for Drax Industry documents in the middle of the night, she did not raise the alarm, but assisted him. Their liaison was soon detected by Chang, Drax's enforcer. Corinne was hunted and killed by Drax's dogs in woods near his chateau.

COUNTRY ESTATE
Drax's palatial home was a genuine French chateau transported brick by brick to California.

HOLLY GOODHEAD
Bond was initially surprised that a top rocket scientist at Drax Industries was a woman. He set aside his chauvinist attitudes when he realized that not only was Holly extremely good at her job, she was also a CIA agent. She preferred working alone and he had to work hard to win her over.

HUGO DRAX

The billionaire owner of Drax Industries affected the languid poise of a latterday French aristocrat. He entertained female guests to his chateau by playing a little Chopin on the piano; he fed his Dobermans steak tartare. He had nothing but contempt for MI6's efforts to hinder his plans.

JAWS

Chang's replacement as Drax's muscle was none other than the indestructible adversary Bond had encountered during *The Spy Who Loved Me* mission. Jaws was determined to get his revenge on 007 – until a little love came into his life.

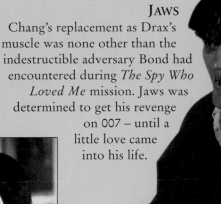

CHANG

Drax's hit man ruthlessly obeyed orders. He was killed by 007 in a fight at a Venetian glass factory.

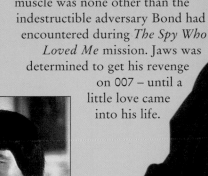

Liquid nerve gas was kept in octagonal jars and placed in pods

POISON GAS

Plans in Drax's safe mentioned a company of his called Venini Glass in Venice. Bond visited the factory and discovered it was a front for lethal chemical experiments. A vial of liquid was accidentally smashed and Bond saw a lab technician die an agonizing death.

DEATH IN VENICE

Drax's killers were still on Bond's tail. One knife-throwing assassin hid in a coffin on a gondola. Bond threw the knife back, and closed the lid on the killer's coffin for good.

Fabric wing stretched over lightweight framework

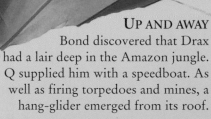

Pilot controls flight direction with bar

UP AND AWAY

Bond discovered that Drax had a lair deep in the Amazon jungle. Q supplied him with a speedboat. As well as firing torpedoes and mines, a hang-glider emerged from its roof.

SNAKE IN THE WATER

Bond landed his hang-glider in the jungle, and came upon a group of girls in white dresses near an ancient temple. A moment later he was tipped into a pool, and attacked by a giant anaconda. He used a hypodermic pen belonging to Holly Goodhead to kill the monster.

SPACE STATION

TEMPLE OF DOOM
Drax's shuttle launch site was concealed inside a Mayan temple in the Amazon jungle.

D EEP IN SPACE orbited a terrifying threat, undetectable from Earth; Drax Industries' Space Station. From it, Drax planned to launch globes of a nerve gas so powerful it could wipe out the world's population. Selected groups of young men and women were already being brought to the station by shuttle. Very soon, Drax's master race would inherit the Earth...

US forces engage Drax's men

Shuttle docking bay

Moonraker shuttle

A WORLD RULER IN WAITING
Drax watched in triumph as his fleet of Moonraker shuttles took off. Each one carried a batch of beautiful people, breeders for his new world.

WHEEL OF FATE
Drax's headquarters was a 260-metre-wide (858 ft) wheel revolving in space. The station's nerve centre and living quarters were located in the central command satellite. Attached to this by inter-connected gangways were six docking bays, where Drax's fleet of *Moonraker* shuttles unloaded their human cargo. The station's radar-jamming system made it invisible from Earth.

THE SEEDS OF DEATH
Drax had discovered a rare orchid in the Amazon rain forest. Exposure to its pollen caused sterility – a possible factor in the extinction of Maya indians who revered the flower. Drax had manipulated the orchid's genes to produce an airborne poison lethal only to humans. "I have improved upon sterility," he explained to 007. "Those same seeds now yield death."

US Marine's space suit had full life-support system

Laser gun

HERE COME THE MARINES
Bond and Holly sneaked aboard and destroyed the station's radar-jamming system. Immediately the US dispatched a force of marines armed with lasers and equipped with power packs for mobility in space.

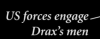

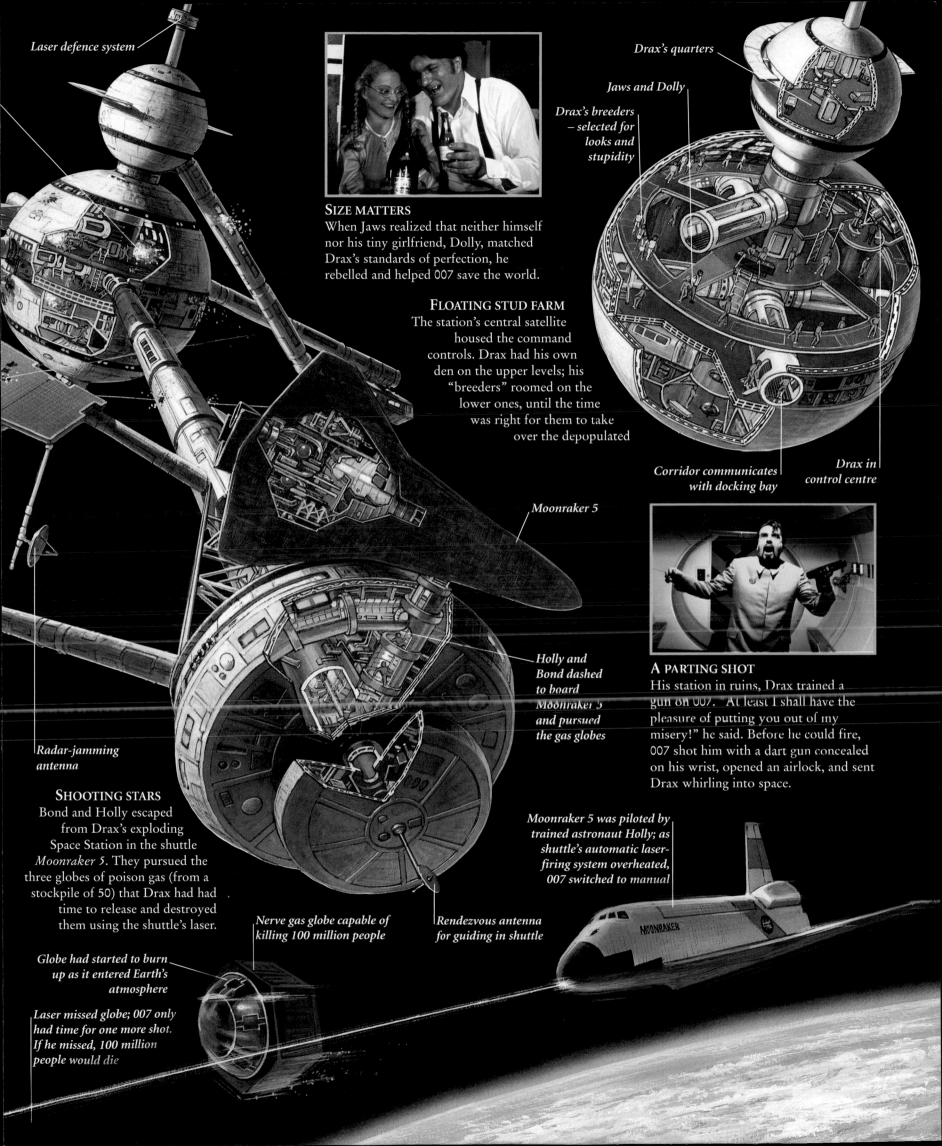

Laser defence system

Drax's quarters

Jaws and Dolly

**Drax's breeders
– selected for
looks and
stupidity**

SIZE MATTERS
When Jaws realized that neither himself
nor his tiny girlfriend, Dolly, matched
Drax's standards of perfection, he
rebelled and helped 007 save the world.

FLOATING STUD FARM
The station's central satellite
housed the command
controls. Drax had his own
den on the upper levels; his
"breeders" roomed on the
lower ones, until the time
was right for them to take
over the depopulated

Moonraker 5

**Corridor communicates
with docking bay**

**Drax in
control centre**

**Holly and
Bond dashed
to board
Moonraker 5
and pursued
the gas globes**

A PARTING SHOT
His station in ruins, Drax trained a
gun on 007. "At least I shall have the
pleasure of putting you out of my
misery!" he said. Before he could fire,
007 shot him with a dart gun concealed
on his wrist, opened an airlock, and sent
Drax whirling into space.

**Radar-jamming
antenna**

SHOOTING STARS
Bond and Holly escaped
from Drax's exploding
Space Station in the shuttle
Moonraker 5. They pursued the
three globes of poison gas (from a
stockpile of 50) that Drax had had
time to release and destroyed
them using the shuttle's laser.

**Moonraker 5 was piloted by
trained astronaut Holly; as
shuttle's automatic laser-
firing system overheated,
007 switched to manual**

**Globe had started to burn
up as it entered Earth's
atmosphere**

**Nerve gas globe capable of
killing 100 million people**

**Rendezvous antenna
for guiding in shuttle**

MOONRAKER

**Laser missed globe; 007 only
had time for one more shot.
If he missed, 100 million
people would die**

FOR YOUR EYES ONLY

A BRITISH SPY SHIP had struck a mine and sunk in Albanian waters. On board was a vital piece of defence equipment, the ATAC transmitter. Bond had to recover it before the Russians got hold of it. The murder of Havelock, a marine archaeologist helping MI6 locate the wreck, gave Bond a lead. He went after the assassin, encountered Melina, the scientist's daughter, on a revenge mission, and discovered another villain, Emile Locque. But who was he working for? A gang boss called Columbo? Or Kristatos, a plausible shipping magnate? Bond and Melina, menaced by killers at every turn, needed some quick answers.

OUT OF THE BLUE
A harmless-looking seaplane appeared in the cloudless Mediterranean sky.

RAIN OF DEATH
The Havelocks died in a hail of bullets from the seaplane that, moments earlier, had delivered their daughter, Melina. She vowed revenge on the pilot, Hector Gonzales.

MELINA HAVELOCK

Throughout the mission Bond was aided by the courageous Melina, whose skill with a crossbow proved vital. Grief and anger over her parents' murder made her a single-minded ally. "I'm half Greek," she explained to 007, "and Greek women, like Elektra, always revenge their loved ones."

OVER BUT NOT OUT
Bond and Melina escaped Gonzales' men in her indestructible 2CV.

Crossbow bolt

REVENGE
Unaware Melina was hunting Gonzales, Bond tracked him to his Spanish villa and was captured. A deadly bolt from Melina's crossbow took out the assassin, allowing 007 to escape.

COUNTESS LISL
The countess' night of passion with 007 – arranged by Columbo to find out more about Bond – had a grim dawn. She died on a beach, murdered by Emile Locque.

COLUMBO

A notorious smuggler, known as "The Dove", Columbo was initially a prime suspect as the man hired by the KGB to snatch the ATAC. He convinced Bond of his innocence and helped him catch the real villain.

EMILE LOCQUE
With the help of Q's Visual Identograph, Bond managed to track down this enforcer from the Brussels underworld. He turned out to be Kristatos' chief hit man, and an utterly merciless killer.

CRASHING CAR
Bond ensured that Locque's fortunes went downhill.

KRISTATOS
For a while, Kristatos managed to hide his treacherous nature behind a veneer of sophistication. Ostensibly a respectable shipping tycoon, he tried to use Bond to murder his smuggling rival, Columbo, while planning to snatch the ATAC for the KGB. Bond was not fooled for long.

SURPRISE, SURPRISE
To prove to Bond that Kristatos was a criminal and in league with the Russians, Columbo took 007 along when he and his men staged a surprise attack on Kristatos' warehouse in Albania.

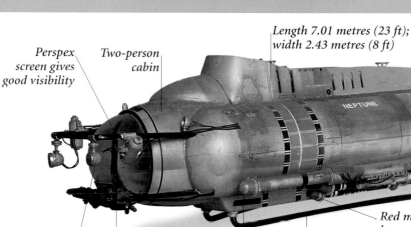

Perspex screen gives good visibility

Two-person cabin

Length 7.01 metres (23 ft); width 2.43 metres (8 ft)

Hydroplane helps raise and lower craft

Propeller

Headlamp for increased visibility in murky water

Pincers for exploring and examining wreckage

Auxiliary oxygen tank

Red marker buoy

Runner protects hull and gives clearance on sea bed

YELLOW SUBMARINE
A mini sub, *The Neptune*, was part of Professor Havelock's equipment in his search for the *St Georges*. Bond and Melina used it to locate the wreck and find the ATAC.

Helmet has four portholes for all-round vision

Powerful pincers

Bond and Melina approach in The Neptune

Articulated joint

THE WRECK OF THE *ST GEORGES*
Bond and Melina soon located the wreck. But their sub was attacked by a diver wearing an armoured diving suit with pincers powerful enough to tear metal like paper.

UNDERSEA EXPLORERS
Wearing scuba gear, Bond and Melina salvaged the ATAC from the wreck.

The ATAC

CAPTURED!
Forced to surface, Bond and Melina were captured. Kristatos tried to feed them to the sharks; they fooled him, but could not stop him stealing the ATAC.

MOUNTAIN EYRIE

Wheelhouse
containing winch
and basket

A solitary guard
spotted 007

THE ATAC
This device, The Automated Targeting Attack Communicator, transmitted a low-frequency signal to the British Royal Navy's submarine fleet. In the wrong hands, the subs' Polaris missiles could have been directed at UK targets.

KRISTATOS HAD CHOSEN his headquarters with care. Sited atop a sheer cliff, like the nest of some huge bird of prey, lay St Cyril's monastery. If the ATAC device was to be recovered from Kristatos' clutches, this seemingly impregnable lair had to be infiltrated. Bond's ally, the smuggler Milos Columbo, knew the place would be well guarded. The best chance of success was a surprise attack from a direction the enemy would not expect. This meant that the cliff had to be scaled. With his experience as a mountaineer, Bond naturally led the assault.

The monastery
possessed some
fine medieval
frescoes

RESISTANCE CENTRE
During World War II, the monks of St Cyril's sheltered Greek resistance fighters from the Germans. It was then abandoned – until Kristatos saw its potential.

UP AND AT 'EM
As soon as Bond reached the summit, he winched his friends up for a battle to the death with Kristatos and his men.

Basket carries
Columbo, Melina
and others to top

APPROACH ROAD
The more usual way into St Cyril's was via a mountain road. Columbo knew that this route would be watched by Kristatos' men.

THE FINAL WORD
The raiding party waited anxiously as Bond began his climb. "Should have brought more of my people," Columbo grumbled. "We are only five men." "And one woman," cut in Melina, crossbow at the ready, rage against Kristatos in her heart.

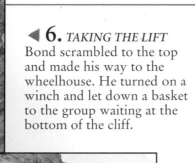

◀ 6. *TAKING THE LIFT*
Bond scrambled to the top and made his way to the wheelhouse. He turned on a winch and let down a basket to the group waiting at the bottom of the cliff.

OUT THE WINDOW
Bond and his allies battled their way through the monastery, searching for the elusive Kristatos. The church's fine stained-glass windows were not the only casualties of the attack.

ERIC KRIEGLER
Kristatos' brutal hit man tried to slow Bond's progress while his boss escaped with the ATAC. 007 was not halted for long, however.

▲ 5. *FIGHTBACK*
As the guard neared one of the last remaining anchors, Bond hurled a knife. The man plunged to his death.

◀ 4.
ANCHORS AWAY!
The guard found a rope, tied it off, and came after Bond, smashing Bond's rope anchors with his pistol butt.

NO ESCAPE
Kristatos attempted to get away with the ATAC, but was stopped by a well-aimed knife-throw from his old enemy Milos Columbo.

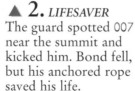
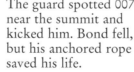

◀ 3.
LACE SWING
Swinging in the air beneath an overhang, 007 improvised a prussik loop with his bootlace and swung himself into the cliff face.

▲ 1. *SUDDEN FLAP*
007's climb was going well until a bird suddenly flew out of a crevice, alerting a guard at the top.

▲ 2. *LIFESAVER*
The guard spotted 007 near the summit and kicked him. Bond fell, but his anchored rope saved his life.

HELLO AND GOODBYE
The KGB's General Gogol arrived by helicopter, expecting to take delivery of the ATAC. Bond threw the machine over a cliff, saying, "That's détente, comrade. You don't have it. I don't have it." Gogol laughed, shrugged, and flew off.

THE ACROSTAR

WHEN A PIECE OF TOP-SECRET US military equipment fell into the wrong hands, Bond was assigned to destroy it at a Cuban air base. This joint CIA-MI6 operation was to be a real hit-and-run mission. Q Branch was well aware that 007 would need to get away quickly, and Q provided him with the fastest, most manoeuvrable vehicle possible: the world's smallest jet, the *Acrostar*.

SPYING OUT THE AREA
Assisting 007 was a CIA agent called Bianca. She found out that a horse trials was to be held near the base. A large vehicle, such as a horse box, would attract little suspicion. Bond disguised himself as a Cuban army officer to infiltrate the base.

Air intake

Aileron

BLOWN AWAY
Bond was captured and driven away. Bianca came alongside in a jeep, towing a horse box. 007 pulled the ripcords on his guards' parachutes and jumped into Bianca's vehicle.

Air-to-air missile

▲ **1. ACTION STATIONS**
As soon as the guards saw Bond fly off in the *Acrostar* they fired a heat-seeking missile at the plane, which tracked it all over the sky.

▲ **2. PASSING THROUGH**
Desperate to escape the missile, 007 flew through a hangar – the very same one where the missing top-secret item of US equipment was stored.

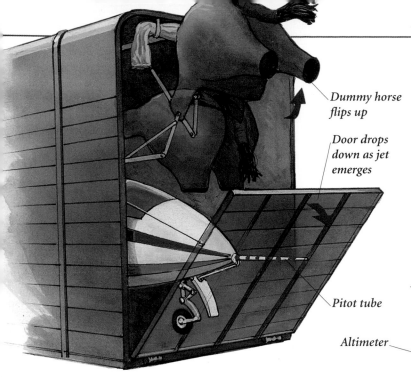

Dummy horse flips up

Door drops down as jet emerges

Pitot tube

UNDER COVER

Bianca's horsebox was not what it seemed. As the door opened, the rear end of a plastic horse flipped up and the *Acrostar* emerged. The jet's wings folded down into position, and it was instantly ready for take-off. Bond leapt into the cockpit.

THE ACROSTAR JET:
SPECIFICATIONS

- **Max. level speed:** 320 mph (512 km/h)
- **Length:** 360 cm (12 ft)
- **Wingspan:** 390 cm (13 ft)
- **Height:** 170 cm (5 ft 8 in)
- **Weight:** 204.5 kg (450 lb)
- **Ceiling:** 9,000 metres (30,000 ft)

Attitude

Airspeed

Engine temperature

Fuel

Altimeter

Cabin pressure

Direction

Horizontal situation

Joystick

THE SMALLEST JET

Powered by a single TRS-18 micro-turbo jet engine, the *Acrostar* was not only fast, but incredibly manoeuvrable – a real acrobat of the air with a maximum dive speed of 350 mph (560 km/h). Its take-off run was 540 metres (1800 ft), and its landing run 240 metres (800 ft).

G-force

Rudder pedals

THE COCKPIT

The single-seater *Acrostar* possessed the standard aircraft dials and controls. Despite its short fuselage, the cockpit could accommodate even a tall man such as Bond in reasonable comfort.

▲ **3. THE EXIT DOOR**

The guards tried to close the hangar's far doors but the *Acrostar* was too quick and nimble. The pursuing missile, however, hit the doors and blew up the hangar and everything in it. Mission accomplished!

Petrol pump adapted for high-octane aviation fuel

Member of Q Branch disguised as Cuban petrol-pump attendant

▲ **4. OUT OF GAS**

The *Acrostar*'s acrobatics drained the fuel tanks. Bond landed on a road and taxied into a petrol station. "Fill her up!" he cried to the pump attendant.

OCTOPUSSY

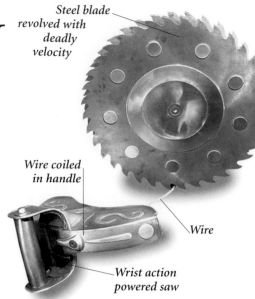

Steel blade revolved with deadly velocity

A MAN IN A CLOWN SUIT – 009 in disguise – had gatecrashed an embassy party and died, a knife in his back… Clutched in 009's hand was a Fabergé egg. MI6 discovered that this priceless jewel was a clever fake, and that another was to be sold at auction. Bond pursued Prince Kamal Khan, the buyer of the egg, to India, and not only uncovered a high-class smuggling racket, but also a plot to start World War III involving a fanatical Russian general. Help came from a beguiling source: the mysterious Octopussy and her travelling circus.

Octopussy's poisonous pet

NO LAUGHING MATTER
MI6's 009 was murdered by Khan's knife-throwing killers, twins Mischka and Grischka.

Wire coiled in handle

Wire

Wrist action powered saw

KILLER YO-YO
A razor-sharp saw operated like a yo-yo by one of Khan's thugs resulted in a messy death for Vijay.

Vijay found a novel way to beat the Delhi traffic

It was business as usual for the street traders

CHASED IN INDIA

The trail led 007 to Delhi, India, where he was assisted by Station I operative Vijay. Bond encountered Khan at a gaming club and won a fortune from him at backgammon using the prince's own loaded dice. Khan was a bad loser, and his thugs, led by Gobinda, Khan's bodyguard, chased Bond and Vijay's three-wheel taxi cab through the bustling Delhi streets.

Vijay posed as a tennis pro – and put his racket to unusual uses

GOBINDA
The immensely strong and silent Gobinda was Khan's enforcer and a remorseless enemy. Time and again, Bond needed all his wits and agility to escape his murderous attentions.

Turning end pushed down plunger to emit acid

Acid reservoir

Ink reservoir

Radio transmitter

Radio receiver

Direction indicator

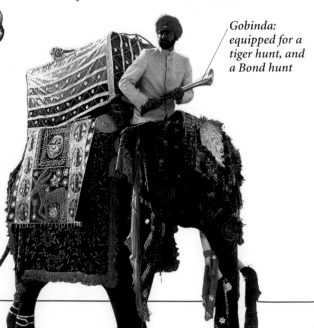

Gobinda: equipped for a tiger hunt, and a Bond hunt

POISON PEN
Q issued 007 with a pen containing a mix of nitric and hydrochloric acid capable of dissolving all metals. The pen's top was a radio receiver compatible with a direction-finder in 007's watch. Q placed a tiny radio transmitter in the Fabergé egg enabling Bond to track Kamal Khan.

GENERAL ORLOV
A fanatical warmonger, infuriated by an improvement in relations between the USSR and the NATO powers, Orlov organized the theft of priceless jewels from the Kremlin. He then sold them to Khan to finance a scheme to start a war by exploding a nuclear device at a US air base in West Germany.

KAMAL KHAN
This unprincipled Afghan prince used Octopussy's circus as a front for his nefarious activities.

OCTOPUSSY AND HER CIRCUS
Secure in her Floating Palace, surrounded by her loyal, all-female troupe – each one a member of her Octopus cult and a skilled acrobat and fighter – Octopussy was an alluring opponent. She knew Bond's presence posed a threat to her smuggling ring, but was grateful to him for allowing her father, Dexter Smythe, a former British agent, to commit suicide rather than face a court martial for murder. As she realized the scale of Khan's deceit, she became a valuable ally as well as a lover.

GREATEST SHOW ON EARTH
When Octopussy was threatened by Kamal Khan in his palace, her circus fighting force sprang into action. His guards were utterly overwhelmed; Khan escaped in a plane, but Bond rapidly brought him down to earth.

Octopussy's jewel smuggling allowed her to live a life of almost unbelievable luxury

MAGDA
The circus ringmaster ran rings around 007, but her tattoo led him to Octopussy.

DEATH TRAIN

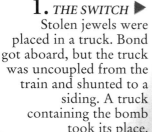

FAST APPROACHING
Octopussy's train steamed out of Karl Marx Stadt, East Germany, heading for the West German border. The nuclear bomb was in the end truck.

BOND DISCOVERED that Octopussy's circus train was not just smuggling jewels stolen from the Kremlin into the West. It had a nuclear bomb aboard, loaded by troops loyal to the renegade General Orlov. He planned to explode the bomb at a US air base at Feldstadt West Germany, during the circus's next performance. European governments would assume the Americans themselves had accidentally triggered the bomb. The confusion would leave the way clear for a full-scale Russian invasion of Europe. Bond had to catch that train!

NUCLEAR BOMB
General Orlov's nuclear device was powerful enough to cause utter devastation over a 20-mile radius. Many thousands of people would die.

1. *THE SWITCH* ▶
Stolen jewels were placed in a truck. Bond got aboard, but the truck was uncoupled from the train and shunted to a siding. A truck containing the bomb took its place.

Guards fire on 007 with machine guns

Departing diesel

Truck used to bring jewels to siding

▲ **2.** *NO SURRENDER*
The jewels were taken from the truck and put in Orlov's Mercedes. Bond confronted Orlov and told him to stop the circus train at the border. Orlov refused to call off his bomb-plot.

General Orlov ran after diesel locomotive

3. *UNDER FIRE* ◀
Orlov's men opened fire and the General gave Bond the slip and ran after a diesel engine that was heading back towards Octopussy's circus train.

Disguised as knife-thrower Mishka, 007 pursued Orlov, but was pinned down by gunfire

4. *COOL RUNNING* ▶
Realizing that the circus train must be stopped, Bond jumps into Orlov's Mercedes, and raced off, dodging obstacles and Red Army bullets.

5. *ON TRACK* ▶
At the East German border, the Mercedes' tyres were ripped apart by steel teeth that rose up from the road. Undaunted, Bond manoeuvred the car onto the rail tracks.

007 got inside rear truck

Crash impact hurled Mercedes into lake

Mercedes' wheel rims fitted rails perfectly

▲ 7. MONKEY SEE
Hiding in a gorilla suit, Bond watched Gobinda set the bomb's detonator by turning a lever clockwise a quarter turn. The bomb was set to go off in four hours' time.

6. SMASH-UP ▲
Bond caught up with the train. Climbing through the sunroof, he leapt aboard as the Mercedes was wrecked by another locomotive.

Locomotive hit car at high speed

Kamal fired through window at 007

A TRAITOR'S DEATH
Orlov was shot at the border by Soviet troops on General Gogol's orders. Gogol had discovered Orlov's part in the jewel-smuggling racket. The Kremlin's jewels were recovered from Orlov's crashed car.

8. ▲
CLINGING ON
Gobinda pursued Bond out of the truck, and Bond hid from him by creeping along the side of the speeding train, hoping to gain entry elsewhere.

▲ 9. EVASIVE ACTION
Bond was spotted and Gobinda went after him, wielding a razor-sharp scimitar. Bond hid beneath a carriage.

10. THE KNIFE MAN ▼
The battle continued on the roof, where Bond faced yet another opponent, the knife-thrower Grishka. They tumbled off, and Bond later dispatched him.

Gobinda

Grishka

007

SEND IN THE CLOWN!
After a hair-raising chase, Bond managed to penetrate the US air base and, disguised as a clown, disarm the bomb with only seconds to go.

A VIEW TO A KILL

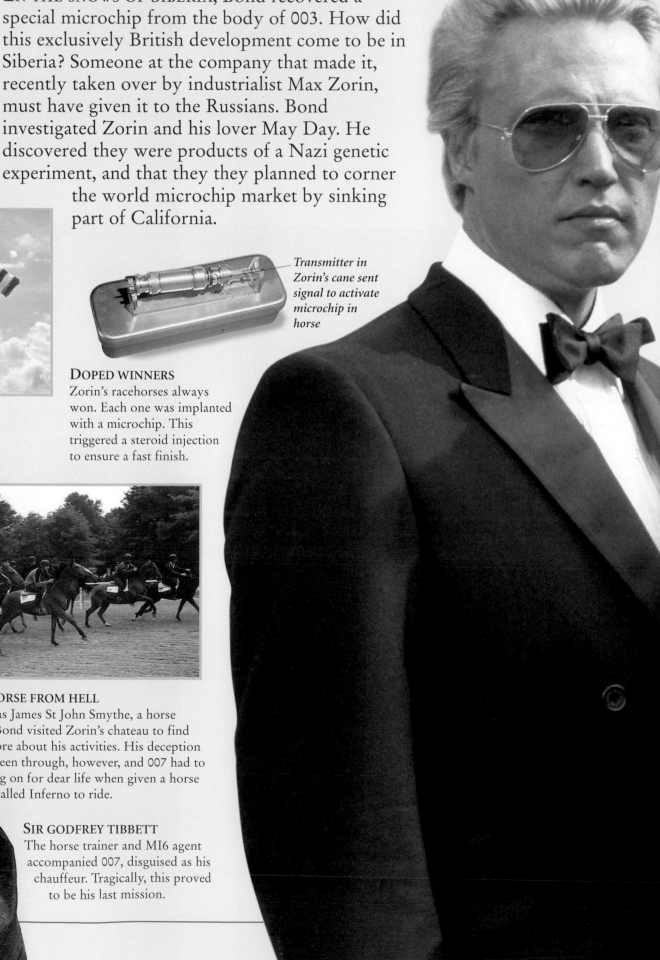

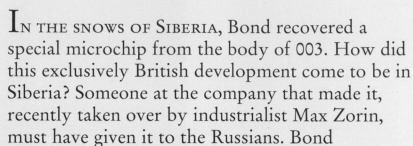

STINGS LIKE A BUTTERFLY
Aubergine, a detective with a lead on Zorin, died before 007's eyes – poisoned by a butterfly during a nightclub act.

IN THE SNOWS OF SIBERIA, Bond recovered a special microchip from the body of 003. How did this exclusively British development come to be in Siberia? Someone at the company that made it, recently taken over by industrialist Max Zorin, must have given it to the Russians. Bond investigated Zorin and his lover May Day. He discovered they were products of a Nazi genetic experiment, and that they they planned to corner the world microchip market by sinking part of California.

FLOATING AWAY
Aubergine's killer escaped Bond by parachuting off the Eiffel Tower.

Transmitter in Zorin's cane sent signal to activate microchip in horse

DOPED WINNERS
Zorin's racehorses always won. Each one was implanted with a microchip. This triggered a steroid injection to ensure a fast finish.

THE HORSE FROM HELL
Posing as James St John Smythe, a horse buyer, Bond visited Zorin's chateau to find out more about his activities. His deception was seen through, however, and 007 had to hang on for dear life when given a horse called Inferno to ride.

SIR GODFREY TIBBETT
The horse trainer and MI6 agent accompanied 007, disguised as his chauffeur. Tragically, this proved to be his last mission.

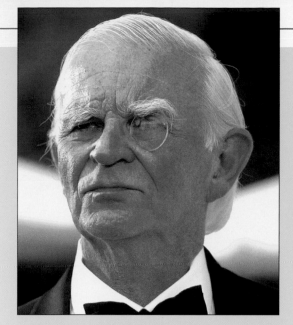

DR MORTNER

An evil genius abetting Zorin, Mortner was a former Nazi concentration-camp doctor. He had tried to create super beings by injecting pregnant women with steroids. All the babies produced turned out gifted, but psychotic.

SCARPINE
Zorin's security chief was almost as ruthless as his boss.

MAY DAY

A product of the same genetic programme as Zorin, May Day was a martial-arts genius and a born killer. Nevertheless, this complex psychopath retained a few shreds of humanity.

IN THE DRINK
May Day and Zorin disposed of Sir Godfrey Tibbett in a convenient lake.

STACEY SUTTON

A geologist working for a California state agency regulating oil and mining companies, Stacey was of vital assistance to Bond in unravelling the details of Zorin's scheme to detonate a bomb in one of his mines and create a cataclysmic earthquake. She also made a very refreshing cup of morning tea.

MAX ZORIN

The super-intelligent, immensely wealthy industrialist had, for many years, been a KGB agent. He now planned to go it alone with a pet scheme to obliterate California's Silicon Valley, source of 80% of the world's microchips. His sophisticated manner concealed a grim secret: he was the result of a Nazi genetic experiment – a biological freak.

PARTNERS IN PSYCHOSIS

Perhaps because of their macabre shared background, May Day and Zorin had a violently intense relationship. But Zorin's lust for power proved greater than his loyalty to his lover.

HIGH-LEVEL CONFERENCE
To present his masterplan, Project Main Strike, Zorin gathered together a group of unscrupulous tycoons for a conference aboard his private airship. Each one of them paid Zorin $100 million to buy into the scheme.

CITY HALL FIRE
To destroy incriminating documents, Zorin set San Francisco's City Hall ablaze and tried to frame Bond and Stacey for a murder. They escaped in a fire engine, Stacey revealing considerable skills as a getaway driver.

HIGH EXPLOSIVE

MAX ZORIN CHORTLED with glee as his airship took off. Any moment now a massive bomb would explode deep underground in his mine. The shock would spark off the biggest earthquake California had ever known. Millions would die, and Silicon Valley, centre of the world microchip industry, would be destroyed. But Bond and geologist Stacey Sutton were about to burst Zorin's balloon for good.

San Francisco Bay

▲ **1.** *THROUGH THE ROOF*
Zorin, Dr Mortner and Scarpine disappeared into a shed. Suddenly fabric billowed through the roof.

2. *UP, UP AND AWAY* ▶
The fabric inflated, and an airship rose from the shed.

▲ **3.** *ABOVE IT ALL*
Flying over the mine, Scarpine and Zorin anticipated "the greatest cataclysm in history."

◀ **4.** *HEROIC DEATH*
In the mine, Bond was trying to dispose of the bomb's detonator. May Day, distraught that Zorin had left her to die, brought it out on a cart. "Get Zorin for me!" she cried to 007. She rode to her death to make sure that the detonator exploded harmlessly in the open air.

Detonator

◁ **6.** *HUNG UP*
Bond grabbed a mooring rope near the airship's nose and was soon swinging over the skyscrapers of San Francisco. "This'll hurt him more than me!" laughed Zorin.

▲ **5.** *SNATCHED AWAY*
Zorin realized his plan was misfiring and thirsted for revenge. He spotted Stacey on the ground, and she was snatched off her feet.

Rails lead straight out of mine

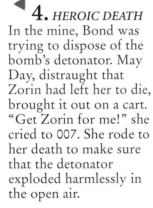

▲ **7.** *ALL TIED UP*
As the airship passed near the Golden Gate bridge, Bond looped the rope around one of the bridge's girders. Zorin screamed for more power, but the airship was securely tethered.

▲ **8.** *KNOCK OUT*
While Bond clambered onto the bridge, Stacey knocked Scarpine out with a fire extinguisher.

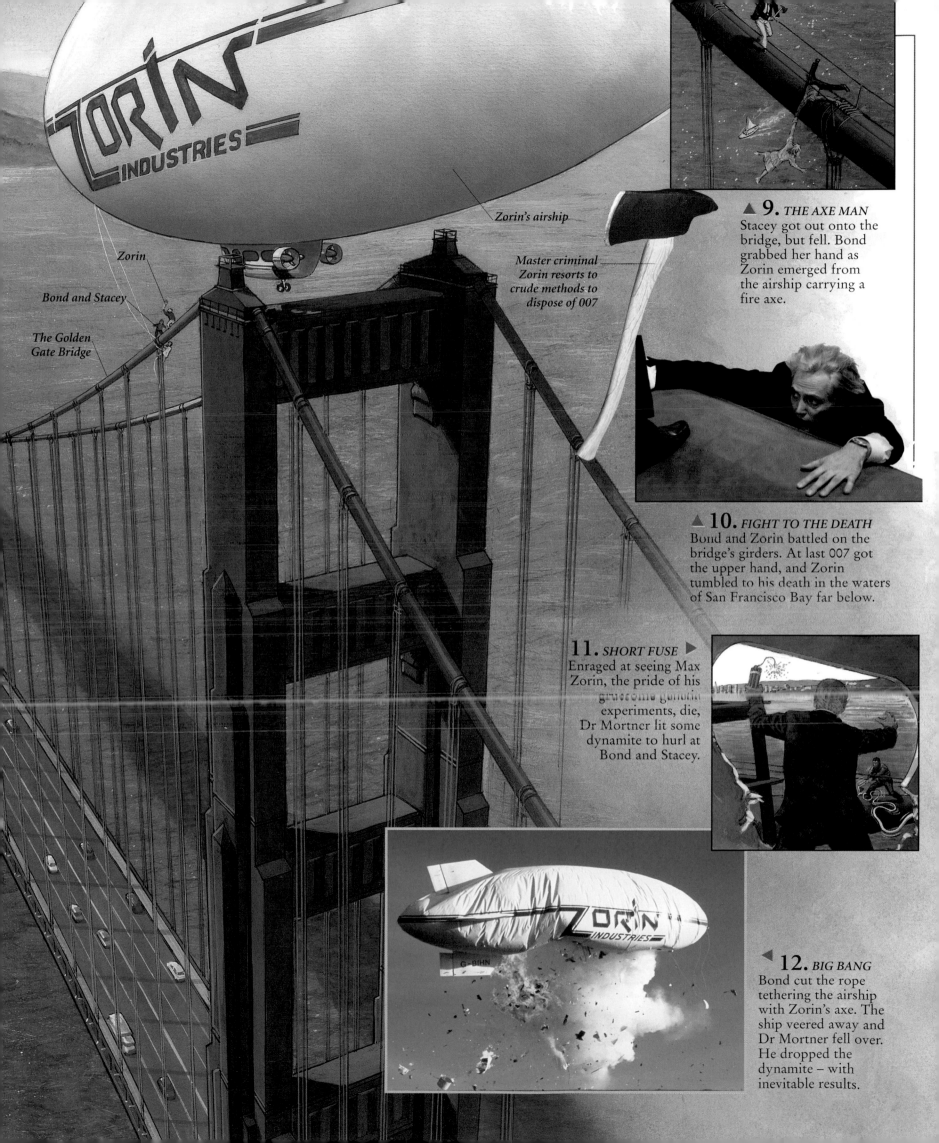

Zorin's airship

Zorin

Bond and Stacey

The Golden
Gate Bridge

Master criminal
Zorin resorts to
crude methods to
dispose of 007

▲ **9.** *THE AXE MAN*
Stacey got out onto the
bridge, but fell. Bond
grabbed her hand as
Zorin emerged from
the airship carrying a
fire axe.

▲ **10.** *FIGHT TO THE DEATH*
Bond and Zorin battled on the
bridge's girders. At last 007 got
the upper hand, and Zorin
tumbled to his death in the waters
of San Francisco Bay far below.

11. *SHORT FUSE* ▶
Enraged at seeing Max
Zorin, the pride of his
gruesome genetic
experiments, die,
Dr Mortner lit some
dynamite to hurl at
Bond and Stacey.

◀ **12.** *BIG BANG*
Bond cut the rope
tethering the airship
with Zorin's axe. The
ship veered away and
Dr Mortner fell over.
He dropped the
dynamite – with
inevitable results.

THE LIVING DAYLIGHTS

WHEN 004 WAS SHOT, and a note, "*Smiert spionam*" – "Death to spies" – was found on his body, it seemed his death was part of a KGB murder campaign orchestrated by General Pushkin. At least that was the story told by Koskov, a defecting Russian general, following his escape from Bratislava. Bond was assigned to assassinate Pushkin, but soon realized that Koskov wanted Pushkin dead for his own reasons. Bond had to gain the trust of Koskov's girlfriend, Kara, to find the truth. He uncovered a plot involving a stone-faced killer, a power-crazed arms dealer, KGB arms cash, and a plane-load of opium.

MI6 assumed the hit man was a KGB agent

SAUNDERS
Bond's MI6 contact in Bratislava and Vienna, Saunders mistook Bond's independent streak for a cavalier attitude to the job. 007 was enraged by his death in a bomb attack at Vienna's Prater amusement park. On a blue balloon was a familiar message: "*Smiert spionam.*"

WHEEL OF LOVE
Kara and Bond first kissed on the Prater Wheel. "Don't think, just let it happen," he said.

Kara's Stradivarius cello, "Mary Rose," cost $150,000 and was bought for her by Brad Whitaker

Bullet hole caused during Bond and Kara's escape from Czech border patrol

OVER A CLIFF
Borne aloft by a parachute, Bond saw 004's killer plunge to his death when his jeep went over a Gibraltar cliff.

KARA MILOVY
A cello virtuoso, Kara's delicate looks belied her courageous nature. She was an innocent, entangled in the web of lies spun by her lover Koskov and his partner Brad Whitaker. Bond initially suspected her of being a KGB agent – and she later suspected the same of him and shopped him to Koskov. But when she and Bond were working together, they made a fine team.

WARNING SHOT
Bond spotted Kara pointing a rifle at Koskov – and scared the living daylights out of her with a single shot. "I only kill professionals. Girl didn't know one end of a rifle from another," he said to Saunders, who felt Bond should have shot to kill. Events proved Bond right – Kara had been posted there to make Koskov's "defection" appear convincing.

Bulletproof shield

BRAD WHITAKER

The architect of a scheme to use KGB arms cash to buy opium from Afghan guerrillas, Whitaker was an arms dealer with absurd military pretensions. In love with war, he had his own museum featuring a pantheon of "great commanders", and re-enacted famous battles with toy soldiers. He claimed to have a fine US Army record, but had been expelled from West Point for cheating. Cornered in his lair, he attacked Bond with a state-of-the-art assault rifle, but met his Waterloo when a bust of the Duke of Wellington fell on him.

GENERAL GEORGI KOSKOV

Smooth-talking and ruthless, Koskov was behind the "*Smiert spionam*" campaign, which he hoped would spread chaos among MI6, and also lead to the assassination of his enemy, KGB chief General Pushkin.

GIVE A LITTLE WHISTLE!

Q provided 007 with a special key ring. Whistle a few bars of "Rule Britannia" and it emitted a puff of stun gas capable of immobilizing an enemy within a 1.5-metre (5 ft) radius for 30 seconds. It also had skeleton keys that opened 90% of the world's locks. A wolf whistle set off an explosive charge.

Arming button

Stun gas discharged here

Plastic explosive

Skeleton keys

PLAYING DEAD

Rubavitch, Pushkin's girl, wept over his bullet-riddled body. But his assassination was a fake – just part of 007's ruse to lull the villains into a false sense of security.

Explosive milk bottle

NECROS

Koskov's hitman was ex-KGB. He caused havoc at an M16 safe house disguised as a milkman, and hurling explosive bottles. Following Necros' one-man raid, Koskov was spirited away from the house to join up with Whitaker at his Tangier base.

SUDDEN STRIKE

Bond persuaded Afghan mujaheddin led by Kamran Shah to attack a Russian air base, allowing Bond to fly off with Whitaker's and Koskov's opium haul.

PACK OF TROUBLE

The opium, worth half a billion US dollars, was packed in sacks disguised as Red Cross parcels. Bond made sure it all went up in smoke!

ASTON MARTIN V8

LOADED WITH ARMAMENTS and specially "winterized" by Q branch with a hard top, retractable outriggers and spiked tyres, Bond's Cumberland grey Aston Martin V8 was a fitting successor to the DB5 and the DBS he drove on earlier missions. It proved its worth when Bond and Kara fled communist Czechoslovakia, under the noses of the Soviet KGB and the Czech police.

MAXIMUM SECURITY
To prevent the car falling into the wrong hands, Q Branch fitted the V8 with a special self-destruct system. A timer gave the driver time to get away before the vehicle exploded.

LUXURY RIDE
The V8 provided comfort and style as well as thrills, with leather seats, air conditioning, walnut dashboard and door cappings, and Wilton carpets. When not listening in to police messages on the radio/casette, Bond drove along to cool jazz.

High-octane fuel tank

Number plate flips up

JET POWERED
For extra thrust, the V8 had a jet-engine booster rocket. Not only did this leave enemy vehicles standing, the blowback from the engine could do serious damage to pursuing vehicles.

Jet exhaust concealed behind rear number plate

Tyre tread

ICE TYRES
Grip is always a problem in snowy conditions, and Q took no chances that 007 would skid off the road by fitting the V8 with special ice tyres. At the press of a button, spikes emerged from the tread of each tyre.

Hydraulic system powered by compressed air pushes spikes through tread

Retractable outriggers, for stability on snow and ice, emerge from door sills

Compressed air reservoir

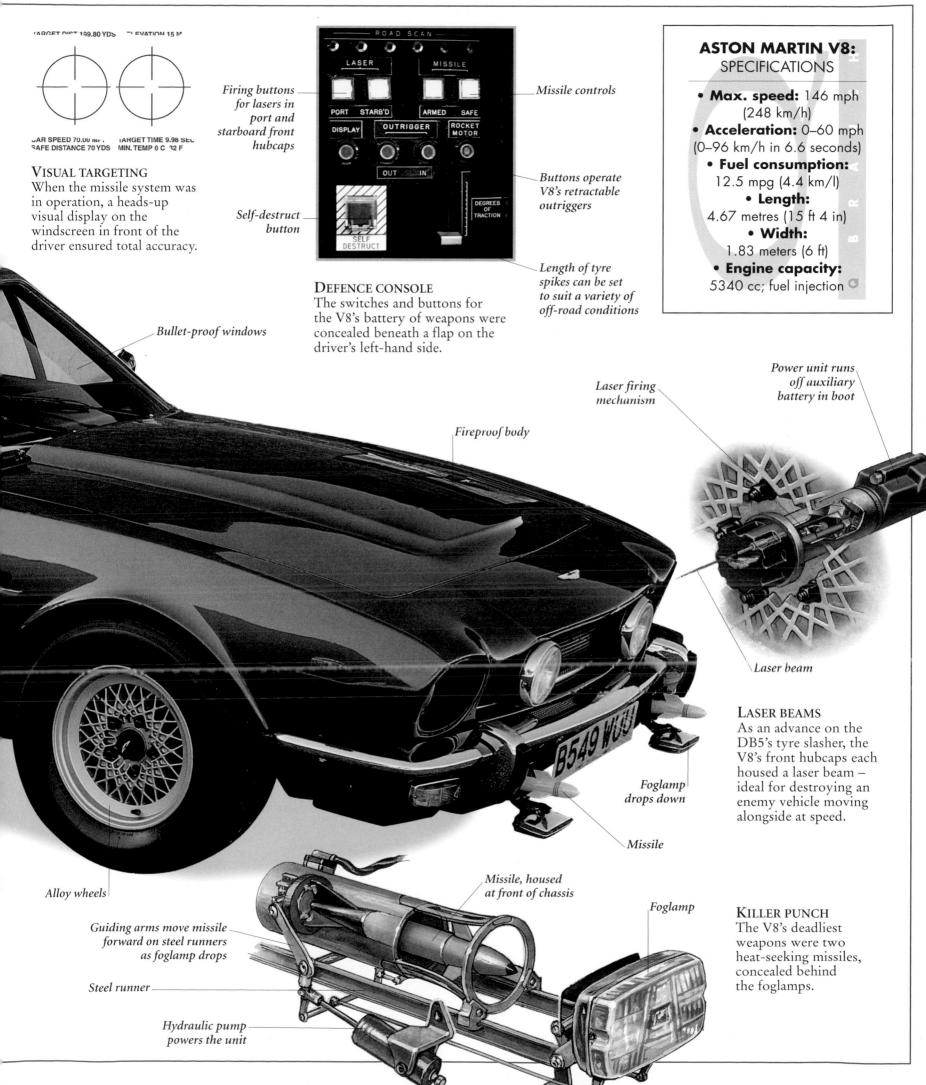

TARGET DIST 199.80 YDS   ELEVATION 15 M

CAR SPEED 70.00 MPH   TARGET TIME 9.98 SEC
SAFE DISTANCE 70 YDS   MIN. TEMP 0 C 32 F

VISUAL TARGETING
When the missile system was in operation, a heads-up visual display on the windscreen in front of the driver ensured total accuracy.

ROAD SCAN

LASER   MISSILE

PORT   STARB'D   ARMED   SAFE

DISPLAY   OUTRIGGER   ROCKET MOTOR

OUT   IN

DEGREES OF TRACTION

SELF DESTRUCT

Firing buttons for lasers in port and starboard front hubcaps

Missile controls

Self-destruct button

Buttons operate V8's retractable outriggers

Length of tyre spikes can be set to suit a variety of off-road conditions

DEFENCE CONSOLE
The switches and buttons for the V8's battery of weapons were concealed beneath a flap on the driver's left-hand side.

ASTON MARTIN V8:
SPECIFICATIONS

- **Max. speed:** 146 mph (248 km/h)
- **Acceleration:** 0–60 mph (0–96 km/h in 6.6 seconds)
- **Fuel consumption:** 12.5 mpg (4.4 km/l)
- **Length:** 4.67 metres (15 ft 4 in)
- **Width:** 1.83 meters (6 ft)
- **Engine capacity:** 5340 cc; fuel injection

Bullet-proof windows

Fireproof body

Laser firing mechanism

Power unit runs off auxiliary battery in boot

Laser beam

LASER BEAMS
As an advance on the DB5's tyre slasher, the V8's front hubcaps each housed a laser beam – ideal for destroying an enemy vehicle moving alongside at speed.

Foglamp drops down

Missile

Alloy wheels

B549 WUU

Guiding arms move missile forward on steel runners as foglamp drops

Steel runner

Hydraulic pump powers the unit

Missile, housed at front of chassis

Foglamp

KILLER PUNCH
The V8's deadliest weapons were two heat-seeking missiles, concealed behind the foglamps.

HAVOC ON ICE

WITH THE CZECH POLICE and the Soviet KGB closing in, Bond had to escape Czechoslovakia with Kara, his sole lead in the Koskov case. He decided to make a break for the Austrian border in his "winterized" Aston Martin V8. Kara slowed him down by begging him to stop and collect her Stradivarius cello. Before too long, the police were hot on their trail.

▲ 1. HERE COMES TROUBLE
Having tuned in to the police band on the V8's radio, Bond was not surprised when a police car started following them.

Laser cut through police car's body

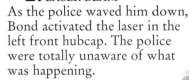

▲ 2. LASER BEAM
As the police waved him down, Bond activated the laser in the left front hubcap. The police were totally unaware of what was happening.

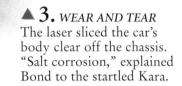

▲ 3. WEAR AND TEAR
The laser sliced the car's body clear off the chassis. "Salt corrosion," explained Bond to the startled Kara.

▲ 4. ROAD BLOCKED
Police had positioned a lorry across the road – there seemed no way past. Unruffled, 007 mentioned that the V8 had some "optional extras". At the press of a button, twin rockets homed in on target.

5. LEAP OF FAITH ▶
The lorry exploded, and Bond drove on. Bullets bounced harmlessly off the V8's bulletproof glass.

▲ 6. BIG GUNS
Suddenly, two armoured cars appeared. One of them fired at the car, but missed. Bond veered down a track that led to an ice-covered lake.

▲ 7. BREAKING COVER
Bond drove into a wooden boathouse and, using it as cover, careered across the ice. Sensing the armoured cars were about to fire, he accelerated out of the shack – just as a shell hit it.

▲ 8. ICE-BREAKER
A lone police car pursued Bond, and a grenade blew off his left front tyre. Bond turned the tables by using the sharp wheel-hub to cut right through the thick ice.

▲ 9. LASER BEAM
The police car foundered in icy water. Bond activated his tyre spikes for extra grip and sped off.

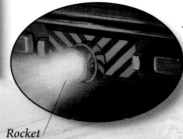

Rocket exhaust

◀ 10. ROCKET POWER
Faced with yet another obstacle – a Czech border post – 007 engaged the V8's outriggers and then its rocket motor.

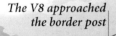

The V8 approached the border post

▲ 11. UP AND UP
The border post's fortifications acted as a ramp, and the rocket-powered V8 hurtled into the air.

Border guards: too surprised to fire

▲ 12. SKI JUMP
The car soared over the guards, and plunged down a hill on its skis.

Border patrol blockhouse

STOP KONTROLA

Ski trooper

◀ 13. CAR SMASH
The V8 finally smashed into some trees. Czech troops on skis saw their chance of making an arrest.

SELF DESTRUCT

▲ 14. SELF-DESTRUCT
Bond pressed the V8's self-destruct button – he and Kara just had time to get clear.

15. HOME FREE ▶
Bond and Kara tobogganed into Austria, using Kara's cello case – it came in useful after all.

LICENCE TO KILL

BULLET HOLE
The hat Bond wore as Leiter's Best Man showed typical wear and tear.

THE SUCCESSFUL CAPTURE of South American drug trafficker Franz Sanchez by Bond and his CIA friend Felix Leiter turned into a nightmare when Sanchez escaped from custody. He and his gang took vicious revenge, feeding Leiter to some sharks and murdering his bride. M refused to allow Bond to pursue a private vendetta against Sanchez, so 007 went Absent Without Leave. With his Licence to Kill revoked by MI6, this time Bond was *really* on his own.

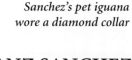

Sanchez's pet iguana wore a diamond collar

WEDDING BELLS
Straight after Sanchez's arrest, Bond accompanied Leiter and his bride Della up the church steps.

FRANZ SANCHEZ
Sanchez expected utter loyalty from his minions and repaid it generously. Despite his confident air, he was prey to fits of murderous violence if crossed. Bond played cleverly on Sanchez's deep-seated fears of betrayal.

BREAKOUT
Sanchez escaped when the armoured truck carrying him to Florida's Quantico jail went off a bridge. Police suspected an inside job.

KILLIFER OF THE CIA
Leiter's treacherous colleague Killifer engineered Sanchez's escape for a bribe of $2 million. Bond later fed him to the same sharks that mauled Leiter.

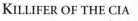

BAD BLOOD
Bond discovered the Leiters' bodies at their home. Della had been murdered. Leiter was still alive, but had been horribly mutilated and lost a leg. A note was pinned to him: "He disagreed with something that ate him."

DARIO

Dario's favourite weapon was a flick knife

Sadistic, streetwise, and exuding menace, Dario was Sanchez's special favourite. He was given the juiciest tasks to perform, such as the vicious murder of Della Leiter.

TOTAL CROOKS

Sanchez's operation used the latest technology to cultivate and export heroin. The cash generated attracted a disparate gang, united by greed.

MILTON KREST

Krest's marine research company provided vital cover and vessels for the transport of drugs to the US. However Sanchez reposed little trust in this shifty, seedy character.

TRUMAN-LODGE

This whiz kid oversaw Sanchez's finances. His nervy personality grated on Sanchez.

JOE BUTCHER

Oily tele-evangelist "Professor" Joe used coded messages in his broadcasts to relay price changes in the drugs market. His Aztec Meditation Centre housed Sanchez's laboratories.

LUPE LAMORA

Sanchez's fiery girlfriend had had enough of his jealous rages and his revolting iguana. She much preferred Bond and helped him to infiltrate her brutal lover's gang.

DRUG HAUL

Bond managed to intercept a load of Sanchez's heroin, which was being transported by a mini-sub belonging to Milton Krest.

PREMEDITATED MAYHEM

At first, Bond gained Sanchez's trust and persuaded him that key associates were on the take. When this subterfuge was detected, Bond adopted more direct methods, such as blowing up the gang boss's desert laboratory.

PAM BOUVIER

An ex-CIA pilot, Pam was the last informant on Sanchez still alive, and thus in deadly danger. Handy with a shotgun, a daring flyer, she proved indispensable to Bond in his war against Sanchez.

TANKER CHASE

BOND KNEW HOW Sanchez had been smuggling heroin into the US: his chemists had devised a method of dissolving the drug in petrol and later reconverting it. Loaded with this explosive mixture, Sanchez's fleet of Kenworth tankers set off from his laboratory. Bond was determined to stop the convoy, and he had a useful helper – ex-CIA pilot Pam Bouvier. Despite being suspended from duty and having his licence to kill revoked, he was resolved to be avenged on the drug czar for his murderous attack on the Leiters.

Bond prepared to jump

Sanchez

▲ 1. FLYING LOW
Bond and Pam, in a light plane, caught up with the first pair of Kenworth tankers, which were accompanied by a car carrying Sanchez.

2. JUMP OFF ▲
Bond perfectly timed his leap onto the top of the front tanker from Pam's plane.

3. CRUNCH TIME ▼
Bond expelled the driver and took the wheel of the lead tanker. The second tanker tried to run him off the road, but was shunted into a cliff.

Bond

Exploding tanker

Ramp

◄ 6. CRUSH HOUR
Bond drove on two wheels towards Sanchez's men. As he righted his vehicle, he crushed the hoodlums' nice white jeep.

Launcher weighed 15.9 kg (35 lb) and had an optical sight

5. ◄
HEAT-SEEKER
Sanchez's man fired; Bond used a roadside ramp to tilt his vehicle. The missile missed, hitting the previously disabled tanker.

Launcher

Sanchez

4. THE STING ▲
Meanwhile, Sanchez had driven on ahead. He met up with two of his men and they prepared to fire a Stinger heat-seeking missile at Bond.

Missile is 152.4 cm (60 in) long, 17.8 cm (7 in) in diameter

7. ▲
UNDER A CLOUD
The hoods shot at the tanker's tyres; it skidded off the road. Before they could get to Bond, Pam crop-dusted them.

9. DIRECT HIT ▲
The trailer hurtled downhill, hitting the leading tanker amidships – with explosive results.

Lead tanker

Trailer filled with petrol

Bond

8. ▼
MOVING TARGET
Bond spotted two more tankers coming up the hill followed by Sanchez's car. He released the trailer from the rig.

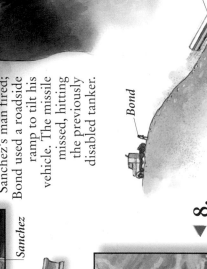

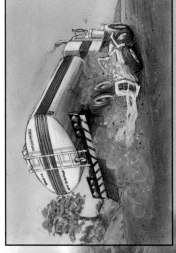

10. THROUGH THE FIRE

Sanchez escaped in the second tanker, and Bond jumped back in his rig to pursue him. When Bond reached the blazing wreck, he lifted the cab up on its rear wheels to escape the flames.

▲ 12. ON TAP

While being shot at by a pursuing car, Bond opened a tap at the back of the tanker. Highly inflammable liquid gushed onto the road.

▲ 11. TOUCHING DISTANCE

Engaging cruise control on his rig, Bond kicked out the windscreen and clambered onto the bonnet as the vehicle closed in on the tanker carrying Sanchez. Bond's rig trundled away and stopped.

13. BURN-OUT

The car chasing Bond, its tyres smouldering after passing the blazing tanker, drove through the petrol on the road and burst into flame. It careered off a cliff, just missing Pam.

▲ 14. CLOSE THING

Sanchez seized the missile launcher. Pam tried to warn Bond. Sanchez blasted a hole in her aircraft's tail.

▲ 15. CUTTING LOOSE

The tanker braked. Sanchez slashed at Bond with a machete, cutting the air-brake pipes.

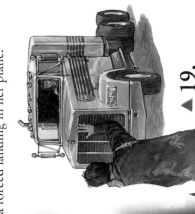

▲ 16. FIRE HAZARD

The tanker rolled forward, petrol gushing from the back. Sanchez, clothes soaked in petrol, slashed at Bond. Meanwhile, Pam made a forced landing in her plane.

▲ 19.

PICK-UP LINE
Suddenly Pam appeared. "What are you waiting for?" she said to Bond. "Get in!"

The lighter the Leiters gave Bond ignited Sanchez's petrol-soaked clothes

▲ 18. FIREBALL

The tanker crashed and burst into flame. Suddenly Sanchez appeared. Bond was a dead man – until he used his lighter to turn Sanchez into a ball of fire.

◀ 17. EMPTY CAB

Having left her wrecked plane, Pam noticed Bond's abandoned rig.

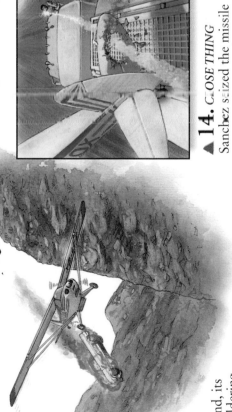

GOLDENEYE

W ORLD SECURITY was imperilled when an international terrorist organization calling itself Janus stole a top-secret Russian weapons system named GoldenEye and threatened to use it to destroy a major city unless paid off. Bond's mission was to recover the GoldenEye, no easy task, for he was faced by a collection of utterly ruthless foes: beautiful, but sadistic, assassin Xenia Onatopp, treacherous General Ourumov, obsessive computer hacker Boris Grishenko, and most devious of all, Bond's former MI6 colleague and friend, Alec Trevelyan.

XENIA ONATOPP
Ex-Soviet fighter pilot and Janus's chief assassin, she killed for the same reason that she did everything else – just for the thrill. She had quite a crush on Bond – it nearly broke his neck!

ATTACK ON SEVERNAYA
MI6 became aware of Janus's activities following the organization's raid on the Severnaya weapons facility in Siberia, during which the GoldenEye was stolen. This disk programmed satellites to fire an electromagnetic pulse that destroyed any object using an electrical circuit. Two of Janus's top operatives, General Ourumov and Xenia Onatopp infiltrated the facility and gunned down the workers. The killers then activated GoldenEye, wiping out the entire facility. Only two computer programmers survived: Boris Grishenko, a nerdy clever-clogs who just happened to be outside at the time, and Natalya Simonova, who witnessed the whole incident.

GOLDENEYE

ON THE RUN
As one of the only witnesses, Natalya was suddenly a marked woman – suspected by Russian intelligence, and a prime target for Janus.

NATALYA SIMONOVA
Natalya was determined to find out who was responsible for the Severnaya massacre. She also possessed the technical know-how to neutralize Janus's scheme to steal the City of London's vast wealth and cover the crime by wiping out all computer records with the GoldenEye. 007, of course, found her irresistible.

ELECTRIC SHOCK
The GoldenEye weapon reduced Severnaya to a smoking ruin in seconds.

BORIS GRISHENKO

ALEC TREVELYAN

Embittered and cynical, Trevelyan bore a grudge against Bond and the entire British nation.

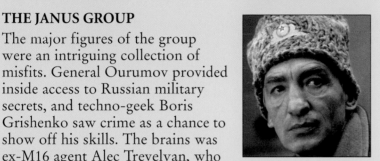

GENERAL OURUMOV

THE JANUS GROUP

The major figures of the group were an intriguing collection of misfits. General Ourumov provided inside access to Russian military secrets, and techno-geek Boris Grishenko saw crime as a chance to show off his skills. The brains was ex-M16 agent Alec Trevelyan, who was believed to have been killed on a mission.

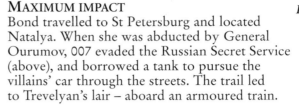

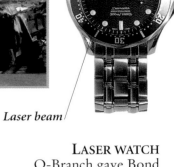

Laser beam

MAXIMUM IMPACT

Bond travelled to St Petersburg and located Natalya. When she was abducted by General Ourumov, 007 evaded the Russian Secret Service (above), and borrowed a tank to pursue the villains' car through the streets. The trail led to Trevelyan's lair – aboard an armoured train.

LASER WATCH

Q-Branch gave Bond an Omega Seamaster watch that emitted a laser beam – useful for cutting through armour-plate.

Bomb activated or disarmed by clicking quickly three times

GRENADE PEN

007's silver ballpoint grenade pen – another gift from Q-Branch – initiated an explosive chain-reaction in Janus's Cuban HQ.

Janus's headquarters

JANUS'S HEADQUARTERS

Thanks to Natalya's hi-tech skill, she and Bond discovered Janus's base in Cuba. From here the group planned to amass vast wealth for itself as well as cause global havoc. But James and Natalya's arrival in Cuba was spotted, and a brutal showdown in the jungle with Xenia Onatopp awaited them.

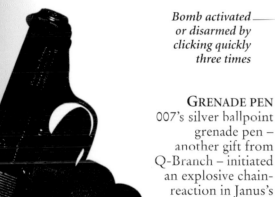

TIGER HELICOPTER

SUPERCOPTER

Proof against electronic impulses, the Tiger was the perfect escape vehicle for Janus's theft of GoldenEye. Onatopp snatched this NATO chopper from under the noses of the French navy.

Trevelyan expected no mercy from Bond – and received none

DEATH PLUNGE

Having scotched Janus's plans, Bond battled with Trevelyan high on a gantry. Trevelyan eventually fell to his death, sneering at Bond and his unswerving loyalty to the Service.

Satellite dish gantry

BAD CHEMISTRY

Bond prepares to jump from top of dam – a 200-metre drop

Laser **Motorized winch**

Piton gun fires steel cable

▲ **1.** *LEAP OF FAITH*
Bond bungee-jumped from the top of the dam, plummeting down towards steel doors set in the roof of the chemical weapons factory.

2. ▶
BREAKING IN
At bottom of jump, Bond fired piton gun. Its steel cable secured him to the concrete roof. Winch on gun hauled him closer, and a laser then bored through a steel hatch.

I F JAMES BOND ever decides to write his autobiography – which, being a loyal servant of MI6 he is most unlikely to do – he would probably admit that few of his special operations have matched the sheer daring of his raid on the Archangel Chemical Warfare Facility in Siberia. It called upon all of his incredible decision-making ability, his refusal to accept defeat, and genius for improvising escapes from seemingly impossible situations. The operation was also to have far-reaching consequences for him and for his partner, Alec Trevelyan (006), on the *GoldenEye* assignment.

Laboratory where chemical weapons are developed

Troops gain access to factory floor by shooting out plate glass window

▲ **3.**
SURPRISE ENTRY
Bond gained access via the factory's lavatory and knocked out a surprized occupant. He then crept down metal stairs towards the storeroom for a prearranged rendezvous.

ALEC TREVELYAN
Alias 006, Trevelyan was a close friend of Bond's, but questions emerged about his loyalty to the Service.

▲ **4.**
CAPTURING 007
Inside the storeroom, Agent 006, who had already infiltrated the factory from a lower level, pretended to capture Bond, who gave the password.

5. ▶
DOWN THE SHAFT
Bond and 006 disappeared down a ventilator shaft into the bowels of the factory to avoid detection by Russian guards.

Ventilator shaft

▲ **6.** *CLOSE TO TARGET*
Bond and 006 exited ventilator in front of door to lab and factory floor.

CAPTURED!
With the operation more-or-less going to plan, 006 was captured and held hostage by Colonel Ourumov. Was there something suspicious about the apparent ease with which 006 was taken?

13. OUT WITH A BANG ▶
As the plane went over a cliff, Bond dived into the cockpit, grabbed the controls, and flew off as the factory exploded.

12. BIKE CHASE ▶
Bond hijacked a motorbike and pursued a plane. He fought the pilot and they both fell out. He grabbed another bike and chased after the pilotless plane.

▲ **11. PARTING SHOT**
Bond jumped on a conveyor belt and started it up. He fired, sending barrels tumbling down on troops.

▲ **10. STAND-OFF**
Using a trolley loaded with explosive chemicals as a shield, Bond edged towards a conveyor belt. Troops were unable to fire.

Pressurized steel barrels filled with highly inflammable chemicals

Opening to outside loading bay

Conveyor belt

Trolley

006 is shot

▲ **9. DISASTER!**
Suddenly the firing stopped and a Russian officer called on Bond to surrender. 006 had been captured. As Bond appeared, 006 was shot.

007 holds off troops with a Kalashnikov assault rifle taken from a dead guard

007 planting other bombs

Digital decoder

Countdown begins

8. COUNTDOWN ▶
While 006 held off troops, Bond attached plastic explosive to chemical tanks and set the timer: 6 minutes to detonation.

05.59

▲ **7. HI-TECH LOCK-PICK**
Using a digital decoder, Bond and 006 entered lab and re-locked the door. But the alarm went off and troops opened fire.

105

DOWNHILL RACE

A BEAUTIFUL WOMAN in a scarlet Ferrari passed Bond's vintage DB5 with a mocking smile – and the race was on. "Who's that?" gasped Bond's wide-eyed passenger, Caroline, an MI6 evaluator. "The next girl," smiled Bond, feeling a familiar tug of anticipation as he floored the accelerator…

1. OUT FOR A SPIN ▶
Bond and Caroline were driving down the Corniche to Monte Carlo.

▲ 2. WHO'S THAT GIRL?
Suddenly Bond's DB5 was tailgated by a red Ferrari. Horn blaring, the Ferrari zoomed past – the driver, Xenia Onatopp, gave Bond a provocative smile.

▲ 3. TOP GEAR
Bond took up the challenge and stepped on the gas.

5. CLOSING IN ▶
The Ferrari jockeyed to overtake on the outside.

▲ 4. INSIDE TRACK
As Caroline screamed with fright, Bond overtook the Ferrari on the inside.

SWEET CAROLINE
Sent out to the South of France by M to evaluate 007, Caroline soon discovered she was on an impossible mission. After the race with the Ferrari, James helped her relax in his own way – there was a bottle of champagne in a secret compartment in his car.

▲ 6. SLOW VEHICLE
Out of sight around a corner, a tractor was chugging up the hill.

▲ 7. IN A SPIN
Confronted by the tractor, the Ferrari spun off, while the DB5 sped on.

▲ 8. DANGEROUS CURVES
Yet the Ferrari caught up again and the two autos burned rubber side by side down the twisting mountain road.

▲ 9. CYCLE LANE
Suddenly one lane was blocked by a group of cyclists toiling uphill.

10. ▲
CLOUD OF DUST
The cyclists collapsed like dominoes as the Ferrari vanished in a cloud of dust.

11. ▲
ONE FOR THE ROAD
Ever the gentleman, Bond waved Onatopp past. Pulling off the road above Monte Carlo, he offered his passenger a glass of bubbly; then he and Caroline commenced a more intimate form of evaluation than M had had in mind.

TOMORROW NEVER DIES

BAD NEWS TRAVELS FAST
Carver made no attempt to disguise his glee that an international incident had marked the launch of his brand-new, 24-hour news network.

SUSPICIOUS MIND
Carver sensed the ambiguity of Paris's claim to "barely" know Bond. From that moment, she was doomed.

THE HEADLINES SCREAMED: "British Sailors Murdered". A British warship, HMS *Devonshire*, had apparently been sunk by Chinese fighters. First with the bad news was the Carver Media Group owned by Elliot Carver. A coincidence? M was not so sure when a false signal received by the *Devonshire* was traced to one of Carver's satellites. Bond was sent to check on Carver – and renew contact with Paris, an old flame who happened to be Carver's wife.

WAI LIN

MI6 was not the only agency interested in Elliot Carver. The Chinese government sent one of its top agents, Wai Lin, to uncover the secrets of his organization. After initial distrust, she and Bond formed an almost telepathic understanding. A martial artist of devastating skills, she preferred to work alone – until she met Bond.

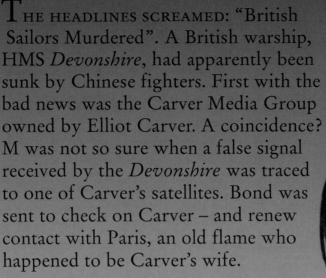

IDEAL PHONE
Bond's mobile phone had a lock-picking system that allowed him to break into Carver's HQ.

PARIS CARVER

"I always wondered how I'd feel if I ever saw you again," said Bond. He soon had his answer – a stinging slap in the face. He had broken Paris's heart years before, and she had consoled herself by marrying Elliot Carver. Yet she still carried a torch for 007, and he had never forgotten the woman who got "too close for comfort".

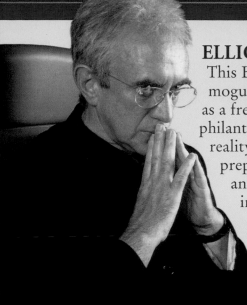

ELLIOT CARVER

This British media mogul liked to pose as a freedom-loving philanthropist. In reality he was prepared to go to any lengths to increase the power of his media empire.

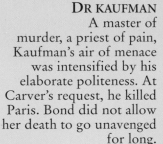

STAMPER
Every tyrant needs a hard man to do his bidding, and Carver chose well. The psychopathic, super-fit Stamper.

DR KAUFMAN
A master of murder, a priest of pain, Kaufman's air of menace was intensified by his elaborate politeness. At Carver's request, he killed Paris. Bond did not allow her death to go unavenged for long.

HENRY GUPTA
The know-how of this "techno-terrorist" was vital to Carver's plans. In many ways, this quietly spoken man was the most dangerous of the magnate's minions.

Stamper's toolbox of Chakra torture

SCIENCE OF SADISM
Dr Kaufman's "hobby" was Chakra torture: inflicting agony by probing the body's pain centres. He passed on his knowledge to Stamper, who was keen to practice on Wai Lin.

ON THE SLIDE
Trapped in a dead end by gun-toting thugs in a helicopter, Bond accelerated the BMW straight at the chopper and skidded underneath its whirring blades.

RUNNING JUMP
Bond and Wai Lin were taken to Carver's Saigon HQ. Carver was writing their obituaries, so they saw no reason to hang around.

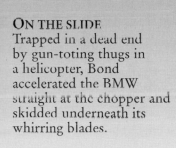

A NEW GUN FOR 007
A bicycle shop in a Saigon sidestreet was a front for Wai Lin's arsenal of weapons and hi-tech equipment. Bond had lost his Walther PPK, so Wai Lin gave him a replacement – the more powerful P99.

BIKER TEAM
On the run from Carver's men, Bond and Wai Lin sped through the Saigon streets on a stylish BMW R1200 – despite being handcuffed together. Wai Lin worked the clutch; Bond accelerated and steered.

IN A TANGLE
Bond destroyed the enemy helicopter by hurling a washing line over the tail rotor blades. The aircraft veered out of control and smashed into a building.

LOST AT SEA

3-D IMAGING
In the control room of Carver's Stealth Ship, an operator watched a 3-D image of the launch of the deadly Sea-Vac drill on a computer screen.

Hms *DEVONSHIRE* was on routine patrol from the Philippines to Hong Kong when it was overflown by two Chinese MiGs, whose pilots claimed the ship had veered into Chinese territorial waters. While the captain and the pilots disputed the point, the *Devonshire* shuddered from stem to stern. Something had holed her below the waterline and she was sinking fast.

TECHNO-TERRORIST
Henry Gupta, the man who virtually invented techno-terrorism, used a GPS Encoder to manipulate the signal from the NAVSTAR navigational satellite and throw the frigate 112 km (70 miles) off course.

NIGHT STALKER
Undetected by radar, the Stealth Ship unleashed the Sea-Vac. The *Devonshire* assumed it was a torpedo dropped by the Chinese MiGs.

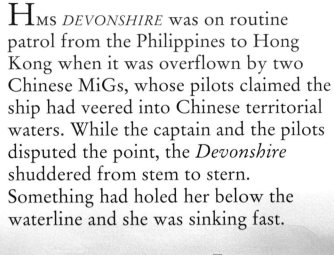

THE GPS ENCODER
This stolen, top-secret CIA device had been bought by Gupta at a weapons "market" near the Khyber Pass on the Afghanistan-Pakistan border.

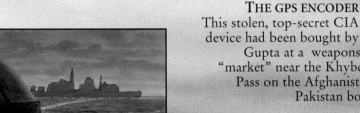

Sea-Vac stops in missile room

Radio room

Bridge

114-mm gun

Harpoon missile system

Radar room

galley

TRAIL OF DESTRUCTION

The Sea-Vac struck in the *Devonshire's* engine room, causing the ship to lose power immediately, and chewed through the ship, smashing bulkheads. Water rushed everywhere. The machine then veered upwards, stopping when it reached the missile and munitions room.

2nd MiG reports back to base

PARTING SHOT

To further inflame the situation, the Stealth Ship fired a missile, hitting one of the Chinese MiGs. The other pilot naturally assumed the missile had come from the Devonshire.

Chinese MiG destroyed by missile from Stealth Ship

MISSILE CAPTURE

When the *Devonshire* had sunk, divers snatched one of the ship's Cruise missiles. When the time came, Carver planned to fire the weapon at the Chinese capital, Beijing, to provoke all-out war between Britain and China.

Tomorrow

LATE EDITION   FRIDAY 11 APRIL 1997   LATE EDITION

BRITISH SAILORS MURDERED

Seventeen machine gunned bodies found

Lynx helicopter

MAKING HEADLINES

After supervising the sinking of the frigate, Stamper ended his night's work by machine-gunning the helpless survivors from the 173-man crew. It all made a great front-page scoop for Carver's newsrag, *Tomorrow*.

Engine room   *Sea-Vac's point of entry*   *Path of Sea-Vac*   *The Sea-Vac*

Wire guides Sea-Vac to target and back to Stealth Ship

REMOTE CONTROL

NONE OF BOND'S CARS can compare for hi-tech gadgetry with the BMW 750iL saloon he drove on the *Tomorrow Never Dies* mission. In addition to a fortress-full of firepower, it could be driven by remote control using a pad hidden in a mobile phone. The BMW also had an anti-theft system that both immobilized the vehicle and delivered an electric shock powerful enough to knock any thief off his feet. In the forlorn hope of getting the car back "in pristine order", Q included a safety feature he hoped would appeal to Bond: a dulcet female voice reminding him to fasten his seatbelt. However, as Q knew only too well, 007 *never* put safety first.

Cutters

CHAIN CUTTER
A steel chain was no barrier to the BMW. At the touch of a button a motorized cutter appeared beneath the bonnet logo that could shear through steel.

Chain cutter beneath logo panel

BEAUTIFUL AND NEW
Q demonstrated how to drive the BMW by remote control by moving his finger around a pad inside a special mobile phone. "Let's see how she responds to my touch," said Bond.

Fingerprint ID

Safe

Spare gun

EXTRA SECURITY
A safe and a spare Walther PPK were in the glove compartment. The lock only responded to 007's fingerprint.

BACKSEAT DRIVING
To drive the BMW, Bond opened up his mobile phone and started the engine by tapping twice on a central pad. He then drew his finger around the pad to steer.

Video screen showed view though windscreen as recorded by video camera behind driver's mirror

ERICSSON

Hinged lid

Buttons activated defence systems

Electrodes gave powerful electric shock

Antenna detached and functioned as a lock pick

Touch-sensitive pad

B:MT2144

12 missiles — — Blast plate

Launcher rose out of tilt-and-slide sunroof assembly

ROCKET POWER
The BMW's most powerful weapon was a rocket launcher system in the sunroof holding 12 heat-seeking missiles.

Spikes neatly stored on top of one another

SHARP SHOCKS
A tray dispensed four-pronged metal spikes to rip an enemy car's tyres to shreds.

Spikes

Rubber solution

Security system electrified handles

Fire-proof and bullet-proof body

Replaceable smoke and CS gas canisters

MAKING SMOKE
A smoke and tear-gas discharge mechanism was concealed behind panels in the trim on each side.

Spring-loaded flap

Compressed-air cylinder

Retractable nozzles

BLOW-UP
The car had re-inflatable tyres – useful when bullets were flying. The system was controlled by 007's phone, or from the dashboard. Rubber solution was sprayed around inside the tyre by centrifugal force as the wheel spun, sealing punctures. Compressed air then re-inflated the tyre.

BMW 750iL:
SPECIFICATIONS
- **Max. speed:** 155 mph (248 km/h)
- **Acceleration:** 0–62 mph (0–99 km/h) in 6.8 secs
- **Length:** 5124 mm (199.8 in)
- **Width:** 1862 mm (72.6 in)
- **Engine capacity:** 5379 cc
- **Transmission:** 5-speed automatic

TEMPER, TEMPER
Unable to gain entry, Stamper made no impression on the bodywork with a flame-thrower.

EMERGENCY EXIT
Pursued by Carver's thugs, Bond was forced to make a speedy exit off the roof of a multi-storey car park – a drop that even the BMW's state-of-the-art construction was unable to withstand.

HALO JUMP

THE MACHINATIONS of Elliot Carver had brought Britain and China to the brink of war. Bond needed to find the wreck of HMS *Devonshire* and discover how and why it had sunk. However a problem remained: how to get to the wreck, which lay between the Chinese and British fleets, undetected by Chinese radar? The only way was to make a High Altitude Low Opening (HALO) jump – a freefall over water from above radar range. Unable to open his parachute until below radar level, Bond would hit the surface of the water with bone-shattering force.

HIGH INJURY RISKS

A major risk of HALO jumps is hypoxia – blackout owing to lack of oxygen. In addition, at very high altitudes, goggles can shatter and eyeballs freeze. The jump carries a 40% risk of serious injury. When Bond hit the water he had to abandon his parachute at once: "90% of deaths are caused by people getting tangled in their 'chutes and drowning," explained his US Army instructor.

Air tube

Radio receiver

Combined oxygen mask and radio

Swimming mask

AIR WALK
Riding in the belly of a USAF Hercules transport aircraft flying high over the South China Sea, Bond entered jump zone.

Aluminium air tank

Flipper strapped to leg

Parachute

Sturdy rubber boots for ankle support on landing

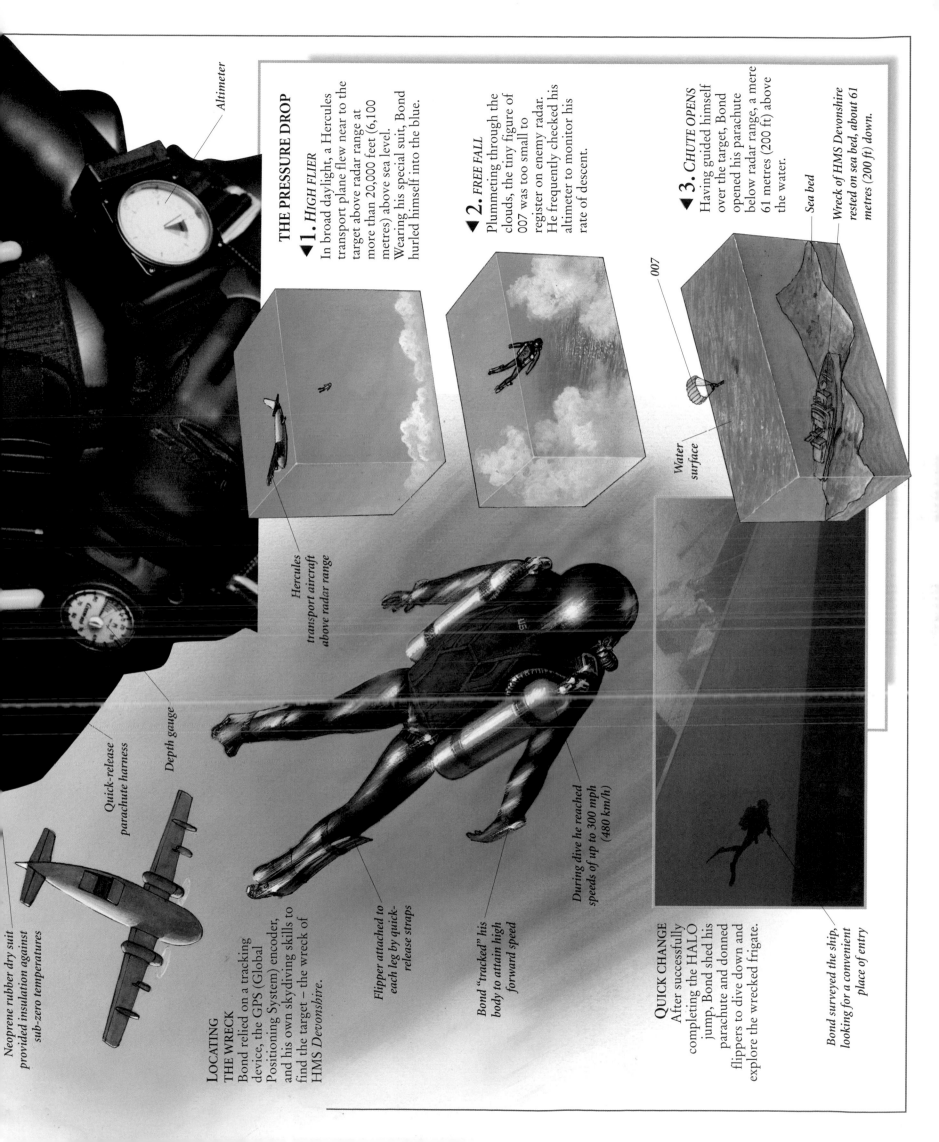

Altimeter

THE PRESSURE DROP

▼ 1. HIGH FLIER

In broad daylight, a Hercules transport plane flew near to the target above radar range at more than 20,000 feet (6,100 metres) above sea level. Wearing his special suit, Bond hurled himself into the blue.

▼ 2. FREE FALL

Plummeting through the clouds, the tiny figure of 007 was too small to register on enemy radar. He frequently checked his altimeter to monitor his rate of descent.

▼ 3. CHUTE OPENS

Having guided himself over the target, Bond opened his parachute below radar range, a mere 61 metres (200 ft) above the water.

007

Water surface

Sea bed

Wreck of HMS Devonshire rested on sea bed, about 61 metres (200 ft) down.

Hercules transport aircraft above radar range

LOCATING
THE WRECK
Bond relied on a tracking device, the GPS (Global Positioning System) encoder, and his own skydiving skills to find the target – the wreck of HMS *Devonshire*.

Neoprene rubber dry suit provided insulation against sub-zero temperatures

Quick-release parachute harness

Depth gauge

Flipper attached to each leg by quick-release straps

Bond "tracked" his body to attain high forward speed

During dive he reached speeds of up to 300 mph (480 km/h)

QUICK CHANGE
After successfully completing the HALO jump, Bond shed his parachute and donned flippers to dive down and explore the wrecked frigate.

Bond surveyed the ship, looking for a convenient place of entry

STEALTH SHIP

VIRTUALLY UNDETECTABLE BY RADAR, the Stealth Ship was Elliot Carver's secret weapon in his plan to stir up international conflicts. From its black hull, the jet-engine-sized Sea-Vac was launched upon the unsuspecting HMS *Devonshire* and a missile fired at a Chinese MiG fighter. Carver's favourite slogan for his media empire – "There's no news like bad news" – fit the Stealth Ship exactly. It was pure bad news.

PLANNED DESTRUCTION
From the safety of the Stealth Ship's control centre, Stamper ensured that the Sea-Vac caused maximum damage to HMS *Devonshire*.

Auxiliary control systems

Observation platform

Bay doors slide back to launch Sea-Vac

Air intake

Wire for guiding an retrieving Sea-Vac

SAM missiles

Starboard engine room: vents cooled engine exhaust

Main missile hatch

Crew's quarters

SEARCH AND DESTROY
Having tracked the Stealth Ship to a bay in North Vietnam, Wai Lin and Bond planted limpet mines on the craft's superstructure. Unfortunately, Wai Lin was spotted and captured by Stamper and the mines removed.

Crew's quarters

Armoury

Door to hull exterior

Entrance hatch

QUICK RELEASE
The Sea-Vac was launched into the sea by being lowered through doors situated between the ship's pontoons.

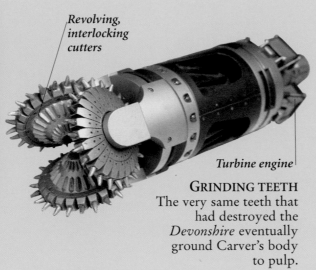

Revolving, interlocking cutters

Turbine engine

GRINDING TEETH
The very same teeth that had destroyed the *Devonshire* eventually ground Carver's body to pulp.

THE SEA-VAC

After visiting the wreck of the *Devonshire*, Bond and Wai Lin realized she could not have been torpedoed (torpedoes explode and do not go around corners). The weapon that sank the frigate was a wire-guided drill with rotary cutters. A video link allowed the operator to guide the drill as it chewed through the ship.

Video camera

SECRET DESTROYER

The Stealth Ship's superstructure had no right angles and was covered with special paint or tape, creating a sleek skin that scattered radar signals. The graphite hull stifled radio transmissions and turned down the heat of the craft's infrared "picture". On screens it showed no larger than a dinghy or a submarine's periscope. The ship's top speed was 48 knots and her armaments included surface-to-air missiles. Concealed CCTV cameras protected the ship from intruders.

Sea-Vac

Radar

Captain's console

CCTV monitor

Stamper checks the ship's course

Satellite navigation tracking equipment

Grenade and detonators were packed in a glass jar

VISIBLE TARGET
To help the British navy locate the Stealth Ship, Bond placed a timer grenade on board, packed with extra detonators. The explosion blew a small hole in the ship, and it became visible on radar at last.

Extra detonators

EXPLOSIVE ENDING
Bond used the Stealth Ship's own rockets to destroy much of its equipment, and its stealth qualities. Meanwhile, British warships closed in for the kill. As the first shells hit the superstructure, the captain called out, "Abandon ship!"

THE WORLD IS NOT ENOUGH

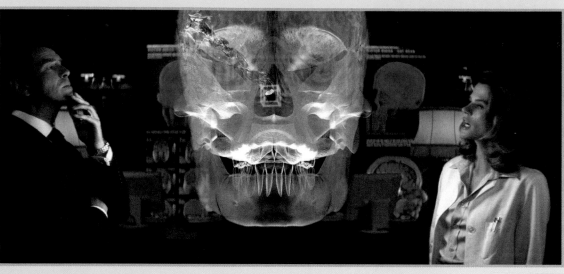

THE MAN WHO FELT NO PAIN
Using a hologram, MI6's Dr Molly Warmflash explained to 007 that a bullet (put there by an MI6 agent) was moving inexorably through Renard's brain, killing off his senses one by one. Soon Renard would die, but in the meantime, unable to feel pain, he was getting stronger every day.

WHEN A BOOBY-TRAPPED case of money killed British industrialist Sir Robert King and blew a hole in MI6's London HQ, M was determined to bring the perpetrators to justice. The prime suspect was Renard, an arch-terrorist with a bullet in his brain and a grudge against King: he had once kidnapped King's daughter, Elektra. M believed Elektra was next on Renard's list and Bond was assigned to act as her "shadow" while she supervised the building of an oil pipeline in Azerbaijan. Yet despite his powerful urge to protect her, there was something about this beautiful, intelligent, wilful woman that aroused his suspicions.

PEOPLE'S CHAMPION
When Bond first met Elektra she was assuring an Azerbaijani priest that the building of her oil pipeline would not destroy his church.

ELEKTRA KING
Her favourite maxim was: "There's no point in living if you can't feel alive." She had once escaped Renard's clutches all by herself. MI6 had failed her then, so she had little faith in 007, now Renard seemed to be after her again.

DAVIDOV
Bond's suspicions about King Industries' brutal security chief soon led him to suspect Elektra herself.

RENARD
This former KGB hitman had set up his own organization and demanded fanatical loyalty; subordinates who failed him killed themselves rather than face his wrath. With the bullet in his brain numbing him to death, he was determined to pull off one last coup against the West. But was he motivated by blind hatred, or blind love?

THE BULL
Zukovsky's shifty, gold-toothed bodyguard was a menace to his boss and an important Renard spy.

FIRE IN THE HOLE
Bond narrowly escaped being blown up by Renard in an underground nuclear test site in Kazakhstan. He leapt onto a cradle and the force of the blast blew him down a tunnel to Dr Christmas Jones and to safety.

Lock-pick springs out

Part of credit card slides back

5343 4828 8801 5902

J. BOND

INSTANT ACCESS
Suspecting the unscrupulous Zukovsky was in league with Elektra, Bond broke into her office using Q's credit card, which opened all doors.

CHRISTMAS JONES
An American physicist overseeing the dismantling of the Kazakhstan nuclear test site, Dr Jones became an invaluable ally of 007's following Renard's theft of a nuclear bomb.

Identity pass

Device for measuring radiation levels

Aluminium case containing Dr Jones' instruments and equipment

X-RAY SPECS
Q's special glasses allowed 007 to see who among the guests at Zukovsky's casino had a gun. And they had other advantages …

Tinted, X-ray lenses

VALENTIN ZUKOVSKY
This Russian gangster always had plenty of tricks up his sleeve. Bond visited his Baku casino to find out about Renard – and suspected his old adversary was hiding something.

THE Q BOAT

SLEEK AND SUPER-FAST, the speedboat was Q's pride and joy. After months of labour the prototype was nearly perfected, the on-board, computerized systems fully operable. Q had told staff that he planned to use it on fishing trips when he retired from the Service. So what were all the armaments for, they wondered – torpedoing trout? When a bomb blew a hole in MI6's London headquarters, Bond jumped aboard to pursue a mysterious suspect, the "Cigar Girl".

GIRL POWER
The suspect had recently posed as a banker's secretary. She had given Bond a cigar, before slaying her boss. Bond was keen to take "Cigar Girl" in for questioning.

NO TIME TO EXPLAIN
Bond sped off in the Q boat, ignoring Q's plaintive cry, "Stop! Stop! It isn't ready yet!" At first, 007 had no idea what an amazing craft it was. As well as its main engine, it had jet engines for extra thrust, could operate in hardly any water, and even function like a submarine for short periods.

DIVE, DIVE!
A barrier closed behind Cigar Girl's launch. Bond activated the Q boat's dive controls, powered under the barrier and surfaced, still hungry for action.

THE Q BOAT:
SPECIFICATIONS

- **Max. speed:** 100 mph (160 km/h)
- **Acceleration:** 0–60 mph (0–96 km/h) in 6 seconds)
- **Engine:** 5.7-litre V 8; 300 Bhp (auxiliary jet engine provides extra thrust)
- **Length:** 4.75 metres (15 ft 6 in)
- **Width:** 1.5 metres (4 ft 11 in)

Air intake; this also ejected when ejector seat was activated

Roll cage

Ejector seat

Windscreen

Spoiler

Aviation fuel tank for jet engine; petrol tank for turbine on opposite side

F-COM/09

Computer port (on each side) for post-operation analysis of boat systems and reprogramming

CLOSE BUT NO CIGAR
Using the power of the Q Boat's jet engine, Bond caught up with Cigar Girl's launch. However Q had not loaded the boat's close-range weapons – machine guns and rockets.

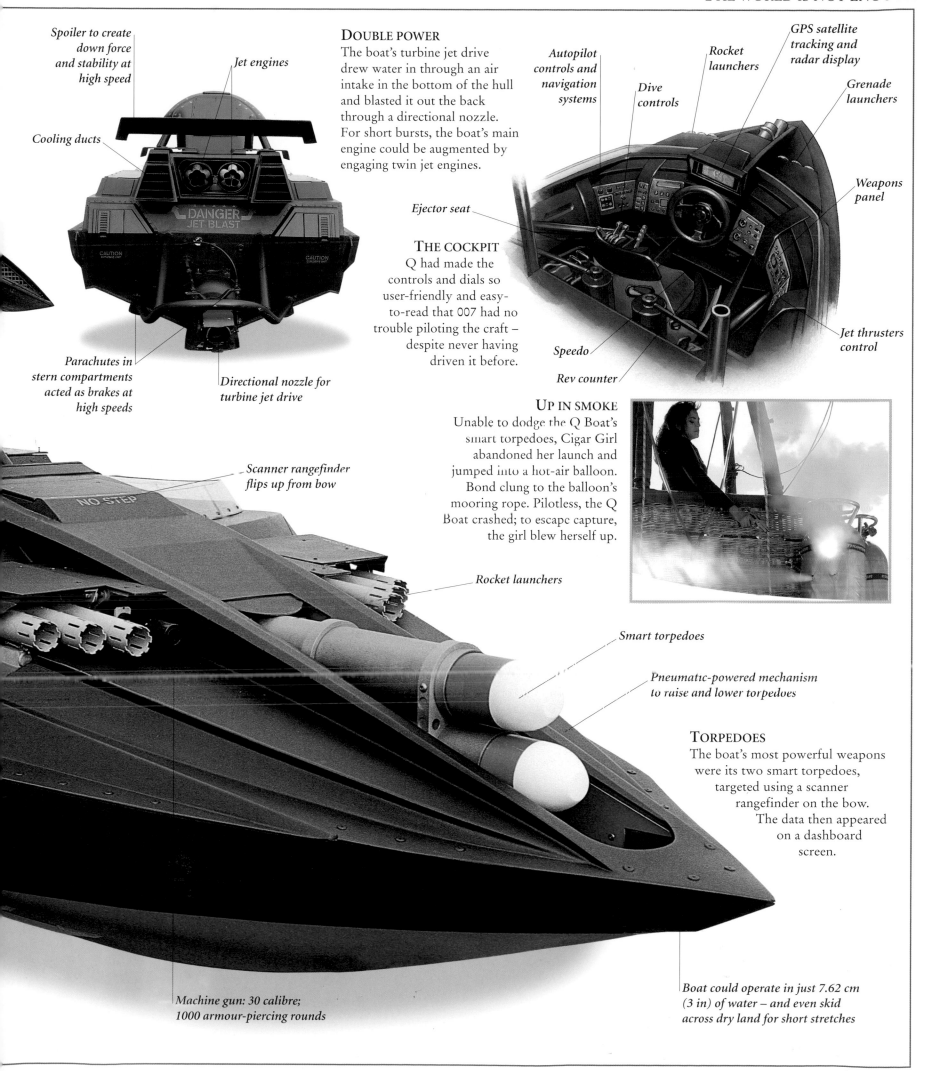

Spoiler to create down force and stability at high speed

Jet engines

Cooling ducts

DANGER JET BLAST

CAUTION

CAUTION

Parachutes in stern compartments acted as brakes at high speeds

Directional nozzle for turbine jet drive

DOUBLE POWER
The boat's turbine jet drive drew water in through an air intake in the bottom of the hull and blasted it out the back through a directional nozzle. For short bursts, the boat's main engine could be augmented by engaging twin jet engines.

Ejector seat

THE COCKPIT
Q had made the controls and dials so user-friendly and easy-to-read that 007 had no trouble piloting the craft – despite never having driven it before.

Autopilot controls and navigation systems

Dive controls

Rocket launchers

GPS satellite tracking and radar display

Grenade launchers

Weapons panel

Jet thrusters control

Speedo

Rev counter

Scanner rangefinder flips up from bow

NO STEP

Rocket launchers

UP IN SMOKE
Unable to dodge the Q Boat's smart torpedoes, Cigar Girl abandoned her launch and jumped into a hot-air balloon. Bond clung to the balloon's mooring rope. Pilotless, the Q Boat crashed; to escape capture, the girl blew herself up.

Smart torpedoes

Pneumatic-powered mechanism to raise and lower torpedoes

TORPEDOES
The boat's most powerful weapons were its two smart torpedoes, targeted using a scanner rangefinder on the bow. The data then appeared on a dashboard screen.

Machine gun: 30 calibre; 1000 armour-piercing rounds

Boat could operate in just 7.62 cm (3 in) of water – and even skid across dry land for short stretches

THE PARAHAWKS

▲ **1.** *SLIPPERY SLOPE*
As they skiied down a mountain, Bond was impressed by Elektra's perfect traverse.

BOND HAD BEEN ASSIGNED to protect Elektra King from Renard. M was taking a personal interest in the case, owing to a close relationship with Elektra's murdered father, Sir Robert King. Bond flew to Azerbaijan, where King Industries was building an oil pipeline. Elektra gave 007 a cool reception, but took him up into the mountains to the pass where the ends of the pipeline would soon meet. It was then that the Parahawks struck.

Auxiliary parachute

◄ **2.** *EASY TARGETS*
They stopped to admire the view. Suddenly the quietness was shattered by the noise of fast-approaching engines.

Headlights

Fixed machine gun

◄ **3.**
DECOY RUN
Four Parahawks suddenly burst over the mountain crest behind them. Telling Elektra to head for a gully, 007 led the Parahawks towards a clump of trees.

Articulated skis

PARAHAWK
Fitted with four articulated skis, this propeller-driven Russian army snowmobile could fly through the air using a parachute to keep it airborne, like a hang glider.

4. ▲
UNDER THE GUNS
Bond zigzagged wildly to avoid the bullets from the pilots' machine guns.

▲ **5.** *HUNG UP*
The leading Parahawk tried to follow 007, but became entangled in the trees.

◄ **6.**
GROUND FORCE
The next two Parahawks landed on the snow, jettisoned their parachutes and pursued the jinking figure of 007.

JUMPING JACK
As well as firing guns, the Parahawks' pilots hurled grenades. Bond just managed to stay one jump ahead.

7. ▶
IN FLAMES
One of the machines smashed into a tree and burst into flames.

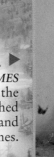

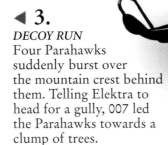

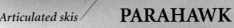

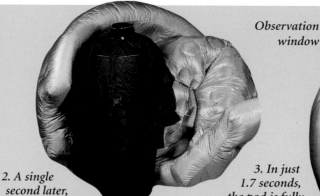

ESCAPE POD
Designed to be concealed within a ski suit or other specialized clothing, the pod, made of aluminium-coated plastic with Kevlar reinforcement, provided protection in a number of situations, including avalanches.

1. On pulling a toggle in the left-hand cuff of the suit, the back panel falls away. Two small steel bottles of nitrogen gas begin to inflate the pod.

2. A single second later, the pod is already half inflated.

Observation window

3. In just 1.7 seconds, the pod is fully inflated into a sealed sphere, with room inside for two people.

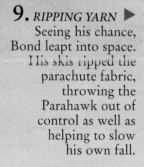

▲ **8.** *FLOATING FREE*
Bond suddenly halted, tricking the other Parahawk into driving over a precipice. Just as he was congratulating himself, the pilot activated the machine's auxiliary parachute and circled back.

9. *RIPPING YARN* ▶
Seeing his chance, Bond leapt into space. His skis ripped the parachute fabric, throwing the Parahawk out of control as well as helping to slow his own fall.

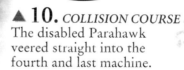

▲ **10.** *COLLISION COURSE*
The disabled Parahawk veered straight into the fourth and last machine.

▲ **11.** *A NEW TERROR*
Both Parahawks exploded in a mass of flame and twisted metal. Bond immediately heard an ominous rumbling sound.

▲ **12.** *SNOWED UNDER*
He just had time to ski over to Elektra before an avalanche, caused by the explosion, engulfed them.

13. *SAFETY FIRST* ▶
Bond activated his ski-suit escape pod, which sheltered them both, and soothed Elektra who was almost hysterical with fear.

DATE WITH DESTRUCTION
Bond arrived in his BMW at a caviar factory owned by Valentin Zukovsky. The head-turning car was spotted and an attack force was in the air in minutes.

FOR *The World Is Not Enough* mission, Q Branch equipped Bond with a customized BMW Z8. Armed with a radar-guided Stinger missile system, the BMW was probably the fastest car Bond had ever been entrusted with. In the hope that this superb vehicle would be returned intact, the car possessed "Dynamic Stability Control". If the driver happened to take a corner too fast, a computer automatically controlled speed and braked the wheels individually, to return the car to a safe trajectory. Unfortunately, not even this state-of-the-art safety feature could protect the Z8 from eventual disaster.

THE BMW Z8

FIRING BUTTONS
The controls for the car's missile defence system were located in the centre of the steering column, next to the manufacturer's logo.

Light signified missile locked on target

Brake pad

Ignition key

Alarm set button in lid

Steering pad

Accelerator pad

Engine management computer

AUTOMATIC AUTO
When danger threatened, Bond could direct the BMW to pick him up by using a remote-control device hidden inside the car's ignition key.

BMW Z8 :
SPECIFICATIONS

- **Max. speed**
155 mph (248 km/h)
- **Acceleration**
0–62 mph
(0–99 km/h) in 4.4 seconds)
- **Engine**
5.0 litre V8; 4941 cc; 400 bhp
- **Transmission**
6-speed manual
- **Weight**
1585 kg (3487 lb)
- **Length**
4.4 metres (14 ft 3.6 in)
- **Width**
1.83 metres (6ft 1.2 in)

HARD SHELL
The car's body was an all-aluminium monocoque space frame, with stressed exterior body panels. Bullet-proof windscreen and armour-plating protected driver and passenger.

King's 'copters
arrived to kill
Zukovsky and 007

CAVIAR FACTORY

Zukovsky was proud of his caviar; the factory was one of his few honest enterprises. Unfortunately its rickety construction could not withstand Elektra King's buzzsaw choppers.

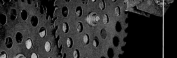

LOCKED-ON AND LOADED

Bond activated his BMW's missile system and got a fix on one of the two attacking helicopters. Moments later it was in flames.

Attachment point

4-stroke engine

TREE TRIMMER

This helicopter-mounted saw is normally used in remote areas of the world to trim back trees where they might interfere with power cables.

High carbon steel saw blades

Wreckage from the rear end of the BMW

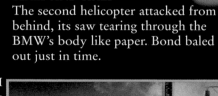

HALF AND HALF

The second helicopter attacked from behind, its saw tearing through the BMW's body like paper. Bond baled out just in time.

Rocket launcher concealed behind air vent

Car carried two Stinger missiles in each wing

ROCKET LAUNCHER

Servo-controlled and fully automated, the Stinger missile system provided a devastating response to enemy action. Radar and laser-scanning target acquisition gave quick and accurate firing.

SPRINT FINISH

Having sawn his car neatly in half, the chopper pursued 007 along a wooden walkway.

V354 FMP

THE MAIDEN'S TOWER

RENARD'S BOAST
Imprisoned in the Maiden's Tower, M was taunted by Renard. He announced that the "bright, starry, oil-driven future of the West", would soon be destroyed and promised that she would die by noon the next day.

DURING BOND'S ENCOUNTER with Renard at the Kazakhstan test site, the terrorist had hinted at an intimate relationship with Elektra. Bond was sure that she and Renard, besides being lovers, were also co-conspirators in her father's death, and in much more. His suspicions were confirmed when M was abducted, and Valentin Zukovsky admitted supplying Elektra with a nuclear submarine. Before Bond could investigate further, he and Christmas Jones were kidnapped. They were taken to the Maiden's Tower, an ancient lighthouse in Istanbul harbour. This was the base for Elektra and Renard's scheme to control oil supplies to the West – and also destroy 8 million lives.

THRONE OF PAIN
Elektra wasted no time in getting Bond exactly where she wanted him – in her torture chair – before confessing that she arranged her father's death.

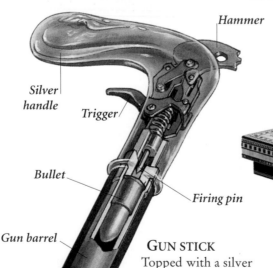

Collar

TORTURE CHAIR
Made of mahogany, inlaid with ivory, Elektra's pride and joy was a beautiful, if macabre, 19th century relic of the Ottoman Empire. The wheel propelled a bolt into the back of the victim's neck until he or she strangled to death.

Wheel

Manacle

Seat

Hammer

Silver handle

Trigger

Bullet

Firing pin

Gun barrel

Foot rest

DEAD SHOT
Zukovsky's attempt to rescue 007 failed when he took a fatal bullet from Elektra's gun. He just had strength for a last shot with his gun stick. It smashed one of the manacles on the torture chair, freeing Bond's arm. 007 didn't waste the opportunity.

GUN STICK
Topped with a silver handle, Valentin Zukovsky's ebony walking stick seemed a typically showy affectation – but it had its uses…

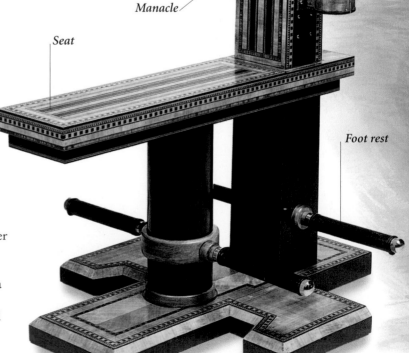

ELEKTRA'S LAIR
The Maiden's Tower hid a nuclear submarine. Renard planned to insert weapon's-grade plutonium into the sub's reactor, causing an explosion that would wipe Istanbul off the map, destroy a key oil pipeline to the West, and give King Industries control of oil distribution through its own pipeline.

THE END OF THE AFFAIR
Elektra was convinced Bond could never kill a woman he had loved. "You'd miss me!" she smiled. A moment later she lay dead. "I never miss," Bond replied grimly.

FLOATING BOMB
Elektra had acquired the Russian sub through Zukovsky's black-market contacts. It was even skippered by Zukovsky's nephew, Nikolai. However Elektra and Renard had no use for a captain, or a crew.

Bond leaps from parapet and boards sub to stop Renard

Elektra King, shot dead by 007

The Bull, shot dead by Zukovsky

Nuclear sub

Elektra's guards' quarters

M

Elektra runs upstairs when 007 gets free

007 locked in torture chair

Zukovsky shoots, freeing 007 from torture chair

Zukovsky's men battle Elektra's thugs

Undersea entrance to submarine pen

GOODBYE LOOK
Elektra and Renard had earlier said a last farewell. The bullet in his brain would soon claim the terrorist's life. "The future is yours," he declared. "Enjoy it."

MISSION TO NORTH KOREA

As dawn breaks, Bond and two other agents, wearing wetsuits, came ashore on surfboards, undetected by North Korean coastal patrols.

Ruthless NK agent Zao was Moon's right-hand man.

A RENEGADE NORTH KOREAN army officer named Colonel Moon was trading weapons for diamonds smuggled from African countries beset by civil wars. Dealing in these "conflict diamonds" was forbidden by the United Nations, and Bond had been dispatched by MI6 to close down Moon's operation. The mission would prove one of 007's most testing assignments.

Compartment in board contained explosives and weapons

007's knife concealed a radio antenna that lured in the smuggler's chopper.

TRADING PLACES
At first all went smoothly: a helicopter taking diamond smuggler Van Bierk to a rendezvous with Moon was intercepted. Bond took Van Bierk's place and the helicopter took off for Moon's camp, piloted by Bond's fellow agents, disguised as NK soldiers.

COLONEL TAN-SUN MOON'S HQ
Colonel Moon's base was in the demilitarized zone between North and South Korea, a flagrant breach of UN regulations. Moon had attended Harvard University in the US, where he claimed to ha ve "majored in Western hypocrisy". As well as lining his own pockets and adding to his fleet of luxury sports cars through his smuggling racket, Moon dreamed of the day democratic South Korea would be ruled by the communist North.

The case Bond carried contained thousands of diamonds smuggled from war-torn African countries. Bond placed an explosive charged beneath the tray holding the gems.

The deal was about to be made, and Bond was waiting his chance to assassinate Moon. Suddenly the Colonel was taken aside by his henchman Zao, who told him that "Van Bierk" was a British agent.

Pretending to demonstrate his tankbuster gun, Moon destroyed the helicopter Bond had arrived in.

CAPTURED!
As soon as the helicopter went up in smoke, killing his colleagues inside, Bond knew he had been rumbled. Could someone at MI6 have betrayed him and his mission? Before Bond could move, Col. Moon's men had seized him and Zao was lining up a firing squad.

Moon was self-serving and utterly ruthless, but in awe of his father

ENTER THE GENERAL
Just as Bond was about to be shot, word came that Moon's father, the General, was on his way to check up on his wayward son. As the young Colonel fled the camp aboard a hovercraft, Bond detonated the explosive in the diamond case. Diamonds flew like shrapnel as Bond broke free.

TORTURE OF FIRE AND ICE
After a hovercraft chase that ended with Colonel Moon's apparent death, Bond was recaptured by the General and held prisoner for 18 months. Disowned by MI6, he was tortured with extreme heat and cold and with scorpion venom to reveal Western secrets, but refused to crack.

Bond's torturer-in-chief was a female NK army officer.

POOR EXCHANGE
Bond was eventually exchanged for Zao, who had been captured on a terrorist mission. Held in military hospital in Hong Kong, Bond faced M, who, believing Bond might have talked, planned to pack him off to the Falklands for "evaluation".

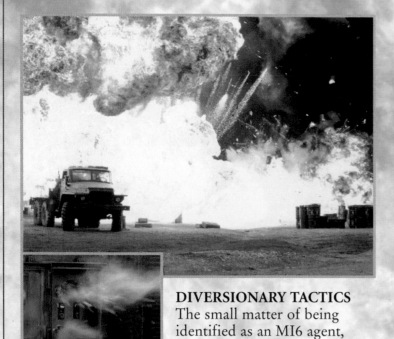

HOVERCRAFT CHASE

BOND'S MISSION to infiltrate and destroy Colonel Moon's arms-for-diamonds racket would not be completed if Moon himself was allowed to escape. Eager to avoid having to explain himself to his disapproving father the General, Moon was making his getaway aboard a transport hovercraft. Bond was soon pursuing him in another hovercraft. He reduced Moon's camp to blazing chaos before speeding over the swampy, mine-infested terrain.

DIVERSIONARY TACTICS

The small matter of being identified as an MI6 agent, apprehended by the enemy and threatened with immediate execution had done nothing to undermine 007's ice-cool resolve. Breaking free from his captors, Bond jumped aboard a military hovercraft and seized the controls. He caused maximum destruction in the camp before shooting out the control panel operating the entrance barrier (inset) to lock it in place and prevent pursuit by Moon's men.

THE CHASE IS ON
Riding a speedy Osprey attack hovercraft Bond set off after Colonel Moon, who was aboard a large transport hovercraft, flanked by two smaller craft.

FIGHTING WITH FIRE
With just a small island of scrub between Bond's hovercraft and his own, Colonel Moon seized a flamethrower.

Moon's camp was in the demilitarized zone between North and South Korea, an area riddled with mines that shoot into the air when detonated and explode.

A sign warned of the danger of anti-personnel mines.

지뢰출몰

THROUGH THE FIRE
Colonel Moon attempted to create a flaming barrier between himself and Bond, but 007 put his foot down and burst through the fire, with little damage to his craft and only superficial burns to himself.

COUNTER MOVE
Moon's much larger hovercraft tried to bump Bond's vehicle off the track. 007 swung his vehicle 180 degrees to slow Moon's craft down and engaged the enemy at close quarters.

AMPHIBIOUS ARSENAL

Riding on a cushion of air generated by centrifugal fans, the amphibious hovercraft is ideal for fast travel in marshy areas. Colonel Moon's transport hovercraft carried an arsenal of weapons, including a mounted minigun and twin surface-to-air missiles on each side.

Minigun fires 100 rounds per second

Twin searchlights for night-time search and destroy missions

OSPREY ATTACKER

Bond jumped aboard an Osprey attack hovercraft to chase after Moon. Bond's Royal Navy training ensured that he had no trouble handling the vehicle.

Twin surface-to-air missiles

Durable neoprene nylon skirt

A riverside temple's bellrope saved Bond's life

HAND-TO-HAND COMBAT

With the two hovercraft locked together, Bond shot Moon's driver and leaped aboard. The previously confident Moon searched frantically for a weapon. As the two faced off, the transport hovercraft knocked the smaller craft obstructing it aside and plunged on, out of control, towards the nearby river.

DIVING FOR COVER

Moon seized a flamethrower. Bond took cover and jammed down on the hovercraft's accelerator. The vehicle careered towards a riverbank crash barrier.

OUT OF THE FRYING PAN...

The hovercraft with Moon still aboard smashed through the barrier and plunged down a waterfall. Bond swung to safety, but his triumph was short-lived: he was arrested on the bank by General Moon and his troops.

DIE ANOTHER DAY

NSA agent Jinx was a superb athlete, swimmer, and diver, as well as being a deadly shot with a Beretta.

M WAS FURIOUS. Not only had Bond escaped from military hospital, news had come through that he had been spotted in Havana, Cuba, on a personal vendetta! Bond had gone "rogue", determined to win back his rescinded 007 licence, and find out who had betrayed him in North Korea. However, before long, M and Bond were reconciled, their agendas the same: to investigate tycoon Gustav Graves, whom Bond believed had made a fortune from smuggling illegal "conflict" diamonds.

PERFECT LANDING
Wearing a parachute emblazoned with the Union Jack, Gustav Graves arrived in style to meet the press gathered outside Buckingham Palace before receiving a knighthood from the Queen. His press agent Miranda Frost was also there to greet him (above).

Allegedly born in Argentina, Graves posed as a patriot to mask his mysterious past.

Bond riled Graves by beating him in a duel at Graves' fencing club. Keen to impress Bond, Graves invited him to a demonstration of his new Icarus project in Iceland.

ON THE HUNT IN HAVANA

Bond encountered Jacintha "Jinx" Jonselle in Havana, unaware that she was an agent for the NSA, a branch of US intelligence. Their paths crossed again in a gene therapy clinic run by Dr Alavarez, who promised to give his clients totally new physical appearances. Bond was hunting the villainous Zao; Jinx's mission was to take out the evil doctor, who was harvesting DNA from healthy donors no one would miss, such as orphans and runaways.

FALCO

NSA chief Falco was convinced Bond had cracked under torture and betrayed important secrets to the North Koreans. He believed the NSA was superior to MI6.

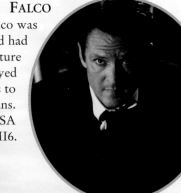

A NEW FACE

Bond found Zao undergoing Alavarez's gene therapy programme. His skin was paler and his brown eyes were now an icy blue, but he was still recognizable. However Zao was not to be captured so easily, and managed to escape 007.

BREAK OUT

Zao crashed through a window and flew off in a helicopter (far right). But he had left a vital clue behind: some diamonds marked with "GG" – the mark of diamond king Gustav Graves.

Jinx's left hand masks a razor-sharp diver's knife hanging from her bikini belt

007 came to realize that gene therapy had transformed Colonel Moon into Gustav Graves

Moon/Graves donned a battlesuit that also controlled his devastating superweapon Icarus

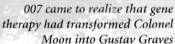

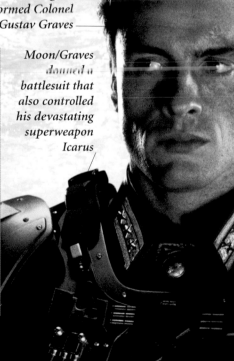

FIGHT TO THE DEATH

Bond and Jinx finally confronted Moon/Graves and his henchman aboard a massive transport plane. As Moon/Graves was about to clear the way for an invasion of South Korea using his Icarus laser-weapon, Bond and Jinx went into action. Moon/Graves died battling 007, while Jinx had a final encounter with triple agent Miranda Frost.

IN Q'S LAB

DURING THE DIE ANOTHER DAY assignment Q's laboratory was in a disused underground station named Vauxhall Cross, near MI6's Thames Embankment HQ. Bond, by now rehabilitated in M's eyes, visited the lab to collect equipment for his mission to Graves's base in Iceland, including a car that could become invisible at the flick of a switch!

Q'S MAXIM
The wizard of MI6 was annoyed by Bond's casual attitude to high-tech weaponry. "As I learned from my predecessor, Mr Bond, I never joke about my work!"

The Vanquish's special features included a console that could "call" the car for a fast pick-up.

The Vanquish's key fob worked by fingerprint recognition.

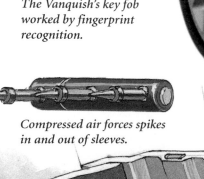

Compressed air forces spikes in and out of sleeves.

GADGETS TO DIE FOR

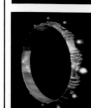
Q supplied 007 with an Omega Seamaster watch with a laser cutter, detonator (operated by twisting bevel), and thermal imager. Bond also received an "ultra-high frequency single digit sonic agitator unit" – a ring that broke bulletproof glass. Bond used it to smash the V12's windscreen and rescue Jinx from her flooded room in Graves's Ice Palace.

EXTRA GRIP
The vehicle's spiked tyres, for use in icy conditions, worked along similar lines to those used on Bond's V8 during the *Living Daylights* mission. This time they would prove even more crucial in saving 007's neck!

Q brought out a flatbed truck on which gleamed an Aston Martin V12 Vanquish fitted with "all the usual refinements" – as well as a polymer skin that rendered the car virtually invisible!

The "adaptive camouflage" polymer skin was applied to the vehicle in sections.

ADAPTIVE CAMOUFLAGE
"Tiny cameras on all sides project the image they see onto a light-emitting polymer skin on the other side," Q explained to 007.

All the V12's windows were bulletproof

SHOTGUNS
Bond tested the efficiency of the car's twin target-seeking shotguns by using them to shoot up the instruction manual!

Magazine

Target-seeking shotguns enabled a wide field of fire

Q'S PRAYER
As Bond went on his merry way, Q cast his eyes to the heavens and murmured, "I wish I could make *you* vanish!"

The V12 Vanquish has a top speed of over 200 mph (322 km/h)

The grille lifts to reveal machine guns and missiles

THE ICE PALACE

GUSTAV GRAVES HAD INVITED the world's press to Iceland to witness the unveiling of Project Icarus, a gigantic mirror orbiting the Earth. Graves's team had created a spectacular temporary residence to house the company: a palace constructed from ice, situated near to Graves's own diamond-mine HQ. Palace guests included Bond, Jinx (posing as a journalist) and fencing champion Miranda Frost, Graves's press agent. Miranda was an MI6 recruit, and 007's sole ally in the enemy's camp.

LIVING THE DREAM
Thrill-seeking Gustav Graves arrived to meet his guests in his latest prototype, an ice dragster (above right), in which he planned to break the land speed record. His maxim was, "You don't chase dreams – you live them."

PALACE PARTY
Before the Icarus launch, Graves threw an elegant party. All the guests were in their finery, including Jinx in a Versace gown. This time, she was posing as "Miss Swift" from *Space Technology* magazine but, whatever she was calling herself, Bond was pleased to see her.

Diamonds were the perfect gems for ice-cool Miranda Frost. Did it occur to Bond where they might have come from?

MIRANDA FROST
MI6 agent Frost was determined not to succumb to Bond's charm. "Sex for dinner, death for breakfast – well it's not going to work with me!" Her resolve lasted, for a while.

The Ice Palace

Graves's base masqueraded as a diamond mine

Plans for the Ice Palace, salvaged by MI6

PROJECT ICARUS
Graves claimed that the mirrors on his Icarus satellite would gently reflect the sun's rays onto the Earth's surface, revivifying desert areas. In reality, Icarus was a superweapon that projected a heat beam of vast destructive power.

Graves's bodyguard went by the name of Mr Kil. "That's a name to die for," quipped Bond. The massive Mr Kil met an untimely end, killed by a laser beam during a fight with 007 and Jinx.

Vlad was Graves's top scientist, and the brains behind Icarus.

Graves, like Zao, had undergone gene therapy to change his appearance. A side effect was total insomnia, forcing Graves to spend an hour each day on his "Dream Machine" to keep sane.

PALACE PRISONER
Miranda Frost, by now open about her allegiance to Graves, gloated over Jinx's imprisonment in the Ice Palace, shortly to be utterly destroyed.

BATTLE OF THE SUPERCARS

GRAVES HAD TRIED to kill Bond using the Icarus laser weapon. Bond had miraculously survived and, now at the wheel of his Aston Martin Vanquish was racing to rescue Jinx from certain death in the fast-melting Ice Palace. Graves's henchman Zao, driving a Jaguar XKR convertible loaded with weaponry, was determined to intercept and eliminate Bond for good.

THRILLS OF THE CHASE
An initial burst from the XKR's rear-mounted machine gun temporarily knocked out the Vanquish's adaptive camouflage. Bond and Zao traded salvoes – at one point, a missile from Zao flipped the Vanquish over onto its roof. Mindful of Jinx's plight, Bond drove right inside the melting palace, pursued by Zao.

SHOWDOWN ON ICE
The ice fields surrounding Graves's base were the perfect setting for a car chase. The world's press had left and the area was deserted, presenting Graves and Zao with the ideal opportunity to dispose of a couple of unwelcome guests.

IN FOR THE KILL
Confident his Jaguar could outgun Bond's Vanquish, Zao had no hesitation in following Bond inside the palace.

RACE AGAINST TIME
Graves's Icarus superweapon had already directed its deadly beam at the Ice Palace, which was beginning to disintegrate as the two cars raced through it.

DODGING CERTAIN DEATH
Zao activated the Jaguar's twin rams, hoping to finish Bond. Fortunately, the Vanquish's adaptive camouflage system returned to life. Bond reversed up an incline.

JAGUAR XKR

Zao was looking forward to getting revenge on 007 following their first explosive encounter. Thanks to his Jaguar's weaponry, he was certain he would be more than a match for MI6's top agent in a four-wheeled duel. He was also confident that Bond's Aston Martin would not out-race him: the XKR accelerates from 0–60 mph (0–96 km/h) in 4.8 seconds and has a top speed of 155 mph (250 km/h).

Missiles housed in door compartment

chains for extra grip on ice

Heat-seeking targeting system.

Rear-mounted machine gun.

Mortars in boot compartment.

Twin hydraulic rams.

A FREEZING DEATH

Bond activated the camouflage system and stopped, his spiked tyres gripping the ice. Unable to see the Vanquish, the bewildered Zao rocketed past, out of control. The Jaguar crashed into a lake of freezing water, once the lobby of the magnificent Ice Palace.

With two well-aimed shots, 007 brought a chandelier crashing down on Zao as he tried to swim free. Bond then rescued Jinx.

BECOMING 007

DETAILS HAVE EMERGED of how Commander Bond of the Royal Navy became James Bond, Agent 007 of MI6. Although battle-hardened in the world's trouble spots, Bond had to learn the spy's subtle arts: how to temper brute force with judgement and how to infiltrate the exclusive circles the world's most dangerous criminals inhabit. There was also the small matter of the requisite number of "kills" to achieve double-0 status...

A MESSY DEATH
One of Bond's first MI6 assignments was to intercept an enemy agent named Fisher (pictured above). Following a vicious life-or-death struggle, Fisher became Bond's first kill.

LICENSED TO KILL
It is accepted in the Service that an agent must kill twice in the line of duty to become a double-0. Dryden, head of Prague section, was unaware Bond was half way there. Guilty of passing on MI6 secrets, Dryden became Bond's second kill. Bond's first target, Fisher, had been Dryden's contact.

LEARNING THE ROPES
Bond had found his second kill much easier than his first. But he would discover that it takes more to be a top MI6 agent than just a steady hand and the ability to shoot straight. He was soon on a more complex mission: to capture a suspected terrorist bomb-maker in Madagascar (see pages 142-3).

HARSH WORDS

M was furious when 007 returned from Madagascar. Bond had caused an international incident by shooting the terrorist bomb-maker MI6 had vitally wanted to question. Bond was determined to prove to his boss that he was more than a "blunt instrument".

GOING IT ALONE

Using M's own laptop, Bond traced a message on the bomb-maker's phone to the Bahamas. The trail led him to Miami airport, where he foiled a plot to blow up an airliner. Impressed by Bond's initiative, M decided to trust her instincts and assigned Bond to ensnare a private banker to terrorists named Le Chiffre at Montenegro's Casino Royale.

SWIMMING WITH SHARKS

The Casino Royale mission meant that 007 had to impersonate a professional poker-player. His colleague, Treasury official Vesper Lynd, taught him how to look the part, replacing his off-the-peg outfit with a bespoke tailored dinner suit. The rest was up to him...

THE DARK LADY

M had warned Bond to keep "emotionally detached" during the Casino Royale mission and Bond, perhaps arrogantly, thought he would have no problem doing so. That was before he met Vesper Lynd. She would show him that life as a secret agent could be even more twisted and tangled than the exotic Algerian love knot she wore around her neck.

MADAGASCAR MISSION

IT SHOULD HAVE BEEN A ROUTINE OPERATION. Bond and Agent Carter were instructed to track a bomb-maker named Mollaka and then take him in for questioning. Carter's behaviour attracted Mollaka's attention and he started to run. Bond pursued the bomb-maker in an explosive, free-running chase. Bond's actions resulted in the elimination of Mollaka and considerable damage to the Nambutu embassy, but did have one beneficial aspect: Mollaka's mobile phone contained a clue to a terrorist plot…

◀ **1.** *THE GIVE AWAY*
Standing amid the crowd watching a mongoose-cobra fight, Carter spotted Mollaka on the move: "He's heading straight for me." As Carter relayed this message to Bond, he touched his earphone. Realizing he was under surveillance, Mollaka bolted.

FREE RUNNER
Mollaka knew that the bomb in his pack would incriminate him as a terrorist. He leapt, sprang and swung through the construction site, revealing amazing skills at *parkour* (free running). Bond refused to give up the chase.

▲ **2.** *ONE SLIP FROM DEATH*
Bond finally caught up with him atop a tall crane looming high above the site. They fought, but Mollaka got free and leaped down to the ground, Bond hot on his heels.

3. *UNDER ARREST* ▶
Mollaka sought sanctuary in the Nambutu embassy. Bond was not going to let diplomatic protocol stand in his way. He charged straight in and collared Mollaka, causing havoc in the process.

◀ **4.** *CORNERED*
Bond was eventually trapped by Nambutu troops in the embassy compound. An outraged Nambutu government official insisted that Bond surrender. Bond appeared to acquiesce, but was determined to have the last word.

5. *OUT WITH A BANG* ▶
Bond shot Mollaka and then fired at a gas canister – with the inevitable results. By the time the smoke had cleared, Bond had vanished clutching Mollaka's backpack.

DEATH OF A PAYMASTER
Bond found a clue on Mollaka's mobile phone: a message, "Ellipsis", sent from the exclusive Ocean Club in the Bahamas by a fixer named Alex Dimitrios. Bond went after Dimitrios, winning his Aston Martin DB5 at poker and seducing his wife, Solange. When she mentioned that Dimitrios was leaving for Miami, Bond followed, sure that Dimitrios was organizing another bomber to take Mollaka's place. Bond caught up with Dimitrios at an exhibition. As the crowd surged around them, the two men fought (pictured right). Bond killed Dimitrios with his own knife.

SKYFLEET SABOTAGE

THE CODE WORD "ELLIPSIS" Bond found in a message on Mollaka's mobile phone set him on a trail to Miami International Airport. Skyfleet was about to unveil its new prototype, the S570, the largest passenger aircraft in the world. Bond was convinced that the aeroplane was a terrorist target. Bond set out to stop this act of terrorist sabotage by any means in his power.

TANKER HIJACK
Disguised as airport police, the saboteur Carlos drove to the refuelling area. After killing the driver, he hijacked a tanker full of fuel.

A FINANCIAL KILLING
The attack on Skyfleet had one motivation: money. The destruction of the prototype would send Skyfleet shares plummeting, allowing those with prior "insider" knowledge of the plan to make a fortune. MI6 suspected that the man behind the plot was a ruthless financial wizard named Le Chiffre.

Carlos clipped a detonator attached to a key ring to the tanker's chassis. He primed the bomb using his mobile phone.

Bond leapt onto the tanker as it sped towards the Skyfleet hangar.

Carlos smashed the tanker though a baggage-handling transporter, sending luggage flying.

CARLOS THE BOMBER

Little is known of the professional saboteur-for-hire whom MI6 has dubbed Carlos. It was subsequently discovered that he had been hired by Alex Dimitrios on the instructions of Le Chiffre, as a replacement for Mollaka, whom Bond had previously eliminated. Carlos was an extremely resourceful and dangerous individual, who would have succeeded in his mission had he not met his match in 007.

UNSTOPPABLE FORCE

The airport police shot out the tanker's tyres but failed to slow it. Some bullets hit the tanker, causing fuel to gush from one side. Bond managed to smash his way into the cab and, after a fierce struggle, force Carlos to bail out. Bond then discovered that the tanker's brakes had failed. He had no choice but to smash through police cars lined up to shield the Skyfleet prototype.

THE WRONG MAN

With his last ounce of strength, Bond swung the wheel and brought the tanker to a juddering halt inches from the Skyfleet prototype. He was immediately arrested by airport police, who thought Bond was the saboteur.

THE FATAL SWITCH

A short distance away, Carlos activated the detonator, which he assumed was still attached to the tanker. He was sadly mistaken. Bond had clipped the detonator to Carlos's belt.

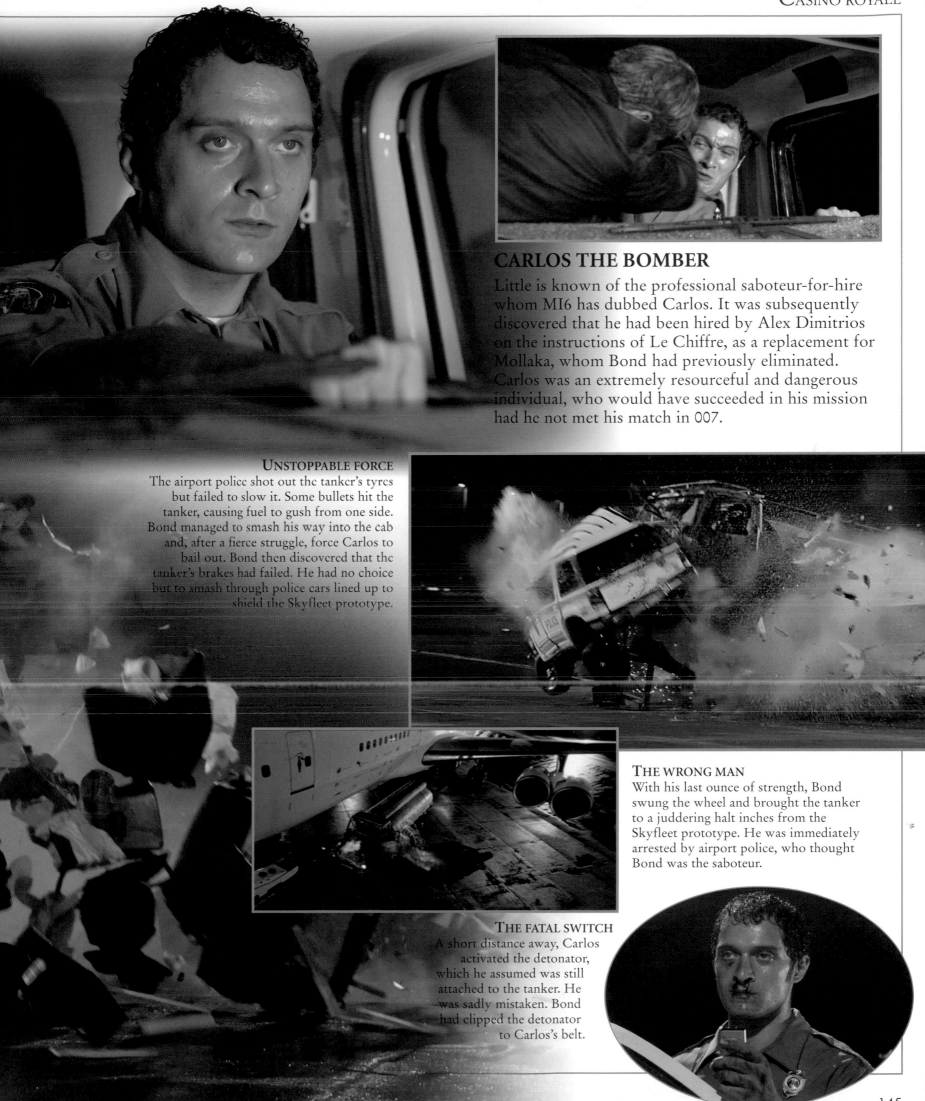

145

Casino Royale in Montenegro provided a suitably imposing setting as Bond faced off against Le Chiffre.

CASINO ROYALE

THE FAILURE of Le Chiffre's plot to blow up the Skyfleet prototype had cost him a vast sum – of other people's money. MI6 heard that he had organized a high-stakes poker game at Montenegro's Casino Royale, and realized he was scheming to win the cash back. Bond was dispatched to defeat Le Chiffre and bring him in for interrogation.

Gambling chips from Casino Royale.

LE CHIFFRE
A private banker to terrorists, Le Chiffre had been gambling with his clients' cash to feather his own nest. He had to recoup his losses fast or he was a dead man.

VESPER LYND
The beautiful agent from the Treasury was ostensibly there to keep an eye on Bond. But she also had her own mysterious agenda.

SOLANGE

The wife of Le Chiffre's associate Alex Dimitrios, she knew nothing about her husband's criminal activities. Unfortunately that did not save her.

HIGH ROLLER

Bond's mission was to gamble for huge stakes – and win! With his ice-cool nerve and knowledge of cards, playing the part of a top poker player came easily to him. To reinforce his cover story, MI6 equipped him with the latest Aston Martin DBS.

A GAME OF LIFE & DEATH

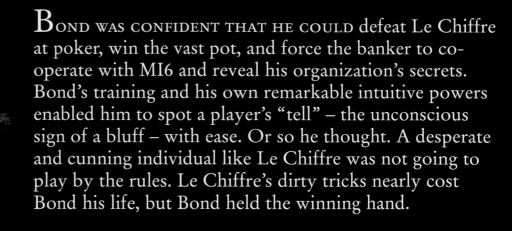

BOND WAS CONFIDENT THAT HE COULD defeat Le Chiffre at poker, win the vast pot, and force the banker to co-operate with MI6 and reveal his organization's secrets. Bond's training and his own remarkable intuitive powers enabled him to spot a player's "tell" – the unconscious sign of a bluff – with ease. Or so he thought. A desperate and cunning individual like Le Chiffre was not going to play by the rules. Le Chiffre's dirty tricks nearly cost Bond his life, but Bond held the winning hand.

RENÉ MATHIS

Bond's Montenegro contact, Mathis won Bond's trust by arranging the arrest of the corrupt police chief. Events later caused Bond to have severe doubts about Mathis's loyalty.

Bond looked like a man who "belonged" at the tables in a tailored dinner jacket courtesy of Vesper. She claimed to have "sized him up" the moment they had met.

STAIRWELL BATTLE

Bond was prepared for a serious test of his nerve and card skills at Casino Royale. He also needed all his speed and strength when two men burst out of Le Chiffre's room and attacked him. Bond was soon forced to add them to the mission's body count.

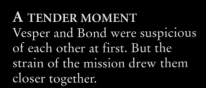

A TENDER MOMENT
Vesper and Bond were suspicious of each other at first. But the strain of the mission drew them closer together.

LEITER'S OFFER

Beaten by Le Chiffre, Bond was about to pursue the villain. However, the CIA's Felix Leiter offered to stake Bond $5 million to buy back into the game.

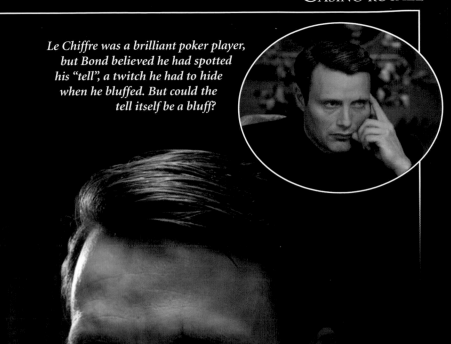

Le Chiffre was a brilliant poker player, but Bond believed he had spotted his "tell", a twitch he had to hide when he bluffed. But could the tell itself be a bluff?

THE THREAT OF OBANNO

During a break in play, Le Chiffre returned to his room. Waiting for him was Ugandan rebel leader Steven Obanno and his lieutenant. Obanno had trusted Le Chiffre with millions of dollars – and he was not going to wait long to get his money back. The Ugandans later turned up dead in Le Chiffre's car, much to his surprise.

VALENKA
Taking a place at the casino bar, Le Chiffre's ice-cool girlfriend was willing to do whatever was necessary to help her man defeat Bond.

Valenka's elegant fingers dispensed death – a fatal dose of digitalis in Bond's martini.

THE FINAL HAND
After recovering from Valenka's attempt to poison him, Bond returned to the table apparently fit and well, much to Le Chiffre's surprise. The final phase of the tournament commenced. Soon four players were vying for a pot worth $115 million. Two players had losing hands, leaving just Le Chiffre and Bond to reveal their cards and decide the winner.

Le Chiffre confidently displayed his hand: a full house of aces and sixes.

Bond won with a straight flush in spades, four to the eight.

DEATH IN VENICE

WHILE RECUPERATING after being tortured by Le Chiffre, Bond and Vesper fell in love. The mission was over, Le Chiffre had been killed by an unknown assassin, the money was safe, and they had each other. Bond now trusted Vesper completely – he was even willing to leave the Service for her. A call from M shattered his dreams. Vesper had transferred the poker winnings to another account and was about to pass on the winnings to Le Chiffre's terrorist associates. Bond was not going to let love blind him to the truth: Vesper was a double agent. Meanwhile, Vesper's guilt at betraying Bond was eating away at her…

SHATTERED PEACE

Bond and Vesper chartered a Spirit 54 yacht for a Mediterranean cruise. Everything was perfect, until they sailed into Venice's Grand Canal. Relaxing on deck, Vesper spotted a face she knew: a killer named Gettler.

THE HANDOVER

Bond saw Vesper hand the cash to Gettler in the courtyard of a crumbling villa.

BETRAYED

"I want to pay for my half of our aimless wanderings," said Vesper, before she set off for the bank. Bond suspected nothing, until M phoned to say that the winnings had not been deposited in the designated account. Bond realized Vesper had tricked him and set off after her. As she gave Gettler the case of money, Gettler spotted Bond and threatened to kill Vesper. Bond battled Gettler and his men, and subsequently killed Gettler.

NO ESCAPE
During Bond's fight with Gettler, Bond shot holes in the inflatable pontoons keeping the villa standing. The entire building began to collapse into the canal. Trapped in a lift cage, Vesper looked on in despair as the bullets flew and the waters rose.

IN THE SHADOWS
Vesper resisted all Bond's attempts to rescue her from the submerged lift cage. By the time he pulled her free, she was dead. The case of money was snatched by an agent of the terror network known as Mr White.

A CHANCE OF REVENGE
Alone on the yacht, Bond received a call from M telling him that Vesper had been forced to work for the network behind Le Chiffre to save her kidnapped Algerian boyfriend. Then Bond saw that Vesper had left him a message: Mr White's number.

QUANTUM OF SOLACE

QUANTUM OF SOLACE continued the high-octane adventures of James Bond begun in the *Casino Royale* assignment. Betrayed by Vesper, the woman he loved, 007 fought the urge to make his latest mission personal. Bond and M interrogated Mr White who revealed that the organization which blackmailed Vesper was far more complex and dangerous than anyone had imagined. Forensic intelligence linked an MI6 traitor to a bank account in Haiti where a case of mistaken identity introduced Bond to the beautiful, feisty Camille, a woman with her own vendetta. Camille led Bond to Dominic Greene, a ruthless businessman and major force within the mysterious organization.

MR WHITE'S INTERROGATION
"The first thing you should know about us," Mr White said, "is that we have people *everywhere*." M and Bond soon realized this was no idle boast.

MAN ON A MISSION
Bond was determined to do his duty – whatever the consequences.

THE HUNTER HUNTED
After capturing Mr White at his villa on the shores of Lake Como, Italy, Bond stowed him in the boot of his car and set off for an MI6 safe house in Siena. White was the sole lead MI6 had on the terror network behind Le Chiffre, Vesper Lynd's betrayal and much more besides. Before long, however, Bond found himself pursued by unknown assailants.

With enemy agents closing in, Bond's Aston Martin cut in front of a lorry.

Amid clouds of dust and flying bullets the cars chased through a marble quarry on the outskirts of Siena.

FRIENDS OR FOES?

Bond's determination to bring down White's shadowy organization threw his personal and professional relationships into turmoil. MI6 colleagues and friends like Felix Leiter were suddenly unsure which side Bond was on, apart from his own. Bond found trust in some unlikely quarters.

Leiter found his loyalty to Bond compromised by orders from the CIA.

M was concerned that Bond was on a personal mission of revenge fuelled by his bitterness at Vesper's suicide. His maverick methods seemed to confirm her worst fears.

M'S DILEMMA

As head of MI6, M was faced with a difficult decision. Under pressure from the British and American governments to bring Bond in, dared she trust 007 to uncover the truth?

MAN OF MYSTERY

Mathis was a prime suspect following the *Casino Royale* mission, but Bond found himself revising his opinion of this fixer supreme.

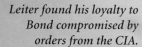

CAMILLE

Bond encountered fiery, free-spirited Camille while pursuing a lead in Port au Prince, Haiti. Soon after they met, she tried to shoot him. They soon came to realize they were on the same side, albeit for different reasons.

AGENT FIELDS

Charged by M to put Bond on the first flight home, she looked like a naive innocent. Bond discovered there was more to MI6's Agent Fields than met the eye. Bond's influence brought out a reckless streak that threatened to prove her downfall.

In Bolivia, Bond and Camille endured a long hot desert walk.

MINEFIELD OF TREACHERY

Mitchell was activated by the terror network to make sure White gave nothing away to MI6.

MR WHITE'S BOAST THAT HIS organization had agents everywhere proved only too true as Bond pursued an MI6 double agent through the medieval centre of Siena, Italy. This was only the beginning – Bond's first step into a minefield of mistaken identity, murderous double-dealing, and political intrigue involving a ruthless business mogul, a would-be dictator, and a woman with her own vengeful agenda. Through it all, as the line between ally and enemy became increasingly blurred, Bond refused to give up on his ultimate goal: tracking down the man responsible for Vesper's act of betrayal…

A TRAITOR IN THEIR MIDST

The emergence of a double agent shocked MI6 to the core. Mitchell had been fast-tracked and trained by M herself. She had trusted him with her life. Questions needed answering – could Bond help provide the answers? M wasn't sure.

Bond pursued Mitchell across the rooftops of Siena.

KILL OR BE KILLED
The chase ended in vicious confrontation. Bond was aware that M wanted Mitchell taken alive, but sometimes it wasn't possible to ask questions first.

154

UNHOLY ALLIANCE
In Haiti, Bond witnessed a strange encounter between businessman Dominic Greene, an exiled Bolivian army officer named General Medrano, and a woman he knew only as Camille. Bond could tell that Camille did not welcome Medrano's attentions.

Bond rescued Camille from General Medrano's odious clutches, hoping she could provide him with inside information about Dominic Greene's various activities.

TO THE LIMIT
Still haunted by the riddle of Vesper's suicide, Bond sought solace in action. Any lead that could help uncover the truth had to be followed to the end, however bitter.

Greene (centre) and his henchman Elvis (left), looked the epitome of suavity as they arrived at the opera house in Bregenz, Austria.

DOMINIC GREENE
The CEO of an international utilities company named Greene Planet, trusted by the British and American governments, Dominic Greene seemed to have a spotless reputation. His eco-friendly business plan, as set out at a fund raiser in La Paz, Bolivia (below) likewise seemed beyond reproach. Bond suspected otherwise.

MASTER OF DECEIT
Bond's journey through a labyrinth of evil led by wicked twists and turns to an apartment in Moscow. It belonged to a man Bond very much wanted to question. A man who was supposed to be dead.

THE MOVIES

To satisfy the public's desire for more information concerning the activities of Agent 007, MI6 has permitted motion pictures to be made of his most spectacular exploits. Thanks to the talents of the Producers, and the many directors, technicians, and actors involved, all of these films were remarkably faithful to the events as they happened, though, in certain cases, the names of characters had to be altered for security reasons. To date, six actors have played James Bond. The real 007 has never disclosed which one he feels has captured him the best.

DR. NO (1962)

Producers
Harry Saltzman, Albert R. Broccoli
Director
Terence Young
Screenplay
Richard Maibaum, Johanna
Harwood, Berkeley Mather
Director of Photography
Ted Moore
Production Designer
Ken Adam
Editor
Peter Hunt
Music
Monty Norman; "James Bond
Theme" played by
John Barry & Orchestra

Cast
Sean Connery (James Bond)
Ursula Andress (Honey Ryder)
Joseph Wiseman (Dr No)
Jack Lord (Felix Leiter)
Bernard Lee (M)
Anthony Dawson (Professor Dent)
John Kitzmiller (Quarrel)
Zena Marshall (Miss Taro)
Eunice Gayson (Sylvia Trench)
Lois Maxwell (Miss Moneypenny)
Peter Burton (Major Boothroyd)
Timothy Moxon (John Strangways)

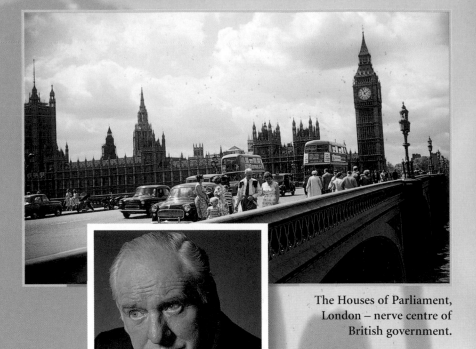

The Houses of Parliament,
London – nerve centre of
British government.

Bernard Lee as the ever-irascible M.

Sean Connery's first appearance as James Bond.

FROM RUSSIA WITH LOVE (1963)

Producers
Harry Saltzman, Albert R. Broccoli
Director
Terence Young
Screenplay
Richard Maibaum, adapted by
Johanna Harwood
Director of Photography
Ted Moore
Production Designer
Syd Cain
Editor
Peter Hunt
Music
John Barry
Title Song
Lionel Bart,
sung by Matt Munro

Cast
Sean Connery (James Bond)
Daniela Bianchi (Tatiana "Tanya"
Romanova)
Pedro Armendariz (Kerim Bey)
Lotte Lenya (Rosa Klebb)
Robert Shaw (Red Grant)
Walter Gotell (Morzeny)
Vladek Sheybal (Kronsteen)
Anthony Dawson (Ernst Stavro
Blofeld)
Fred Haggerty (Krilencu)
Bernard Lee (M)
Desmond Llewelyn (Major Boothroyd)
Lois Maxwell (Miss Moneypenny)
Eunice Gayson (Sylvia Trench)
Aliza Gur (Vida)
Martine Beswick (Zora)
Nadja Regin (Kerim Bey's girl)

The Orient
Express dining
car – where Bond
and Tanya share a
table with
SPECTRE killer
Red Grant.

A Jamaican beach – a paradise tainted by the
radioactivity from Dr No's lair.

Ursula Andress as Honey Ryder.

GOLDFINGER (1964)

Producers
Harry Saltzman, Albert R. Broccoli
Director
Guy Hamilton
Screenplay
Richard Maibaum, Paul Dehn
Director of photography
Ted Moore
Production Designer
Ken Adam
Editor
Peter Hunt
Music
John Barry
Title Song
Lyrics by Leslie Bricusse,
Anthony Newley,
sung by Shirley Bassey

Cast
Sean Connery (James Bond)
Honor Blackman (Pussy Galore)
Gert Frobe (Auric Goldfinger)
Harold Sakata (Oddjob)
Bernard Lee (M)
Lois Maxwell (Miss Moneypenny)
Desmond Llewelyn (Q)
Cec Linder (Felix Leiter)
Shirley Eaton (Jill Masterson)
Tania Mallet (Tilly Masterson)
Martin Benson (Mr Solo)
Michael Mellinger (Kisch)
Burt Kwouk (Mr Ling)

A coral reef off the coast of the Bahamas – danger waters for 007.

Martine Beswick as MI6 agent Paula Caplan, a Largo victim.

Miami – where Goldfinger has his first brush with Bond.

Shirley Eaton as Jill Masterson – before Oddjob's paint job.

Cec Linder as Bond's faithful CIA ally Felix Leiter.

THUNDERBALL (1965)

Executive Producers
Harry Saltzman, Albert R. Broccoli
Producer
Kevin McClory for Eon Productions
Director
Terence Young
Screenplay
Richard Maibaum, John Hopkins, based
on an original story
by Kevin McClory, Jack Whittingham
and Ian Fleming
Director of Photography
Ted Moore
Production Designer
Ken Adam
Supervising Editor
Peter Hunt
Music
John Barry
Title Song
Lyrics by Don Black, sung by Tom Jones

Cast
Sean Connery (James Bond)
Claudine Auger (Domino Derval)
Adolfo Celi (Emilio Largo)
Luciana Paluzzi (Fiona Volpe)
Guy Dolcman (Count Lippe)
Philip Locke (Vargas)
Paul Stassino (Angelo Palazzi)
George Pravda (Ladislav Kutze)
Anthony Dawson (Ernst Stavro Blofeld)
Rik Van Nutter (Felix Leiter)
Earl Cameron (Pinder)
Bernard Lee (M)
Lois Maxwell (Miss Moneypenny)
Desmond Llewelyn (Q)
Martine Beswick (Paula Caplan)
Molly Peters (Patricia Fearing)

Molly Peters as therapist Patricia Fearing of the Shrublands clinic, Bond's choice for rest and relaxation.

Himeji castle – where Tiger Tanaka has his Ninja training school.

YOU ONLY LIVE TWICE (1967)

Producers
Harry Saltzman, Albert R. Broccoli
Director
Lewis Gilbert
Screenplay
Roald Dahl
Director of Photography
Freddie Young
Production Designer
Ken Adam
Editor
Thelma Connell
Music
John Barry
Title Song
Lyrics by Leslie Bricusse, sung by Nancy Sinatra

Cast
Sean Connery (James Bond)
Donald Pleasence (Ernst Stavro Blofeld)
Karin Dor (Helga Brandt)
Mie Hama (Kissy Suzuki)
Akiko Wakabayashi (Aki)
Tetsuro Tamba (Tiger Tanaka)
Teru Shimada (Mr Osato)
Bernard Lee (M)
Lois Maxwell (Miss Moneypenny)
Desmond Llewelyn (Q)
Charles Gray (Henderson)

Lois Maxwell, charm personified as M's secretary Miss Moneypenny.

Hong Kong — where Bond lives once.

ON HER MAJESTY'S SECRET SERVICE (1969)

Producers
Harry Saltzman, Albert R. Broccoli
Director
Peter Hunt
Screenplay
Richard Maibaum
Director of photography
Michael Reed
Production Designer
Syd Cain
Special Effects
John Stears
Editor
John Glen
Music
John Barry
Title Song
"We Have All The Time In The World",
lyrics by Hal David, sung by Louis Armstrong

Cast
George Lazenby (James Bond)
Diana Rigg (Tracy Di Vicenzo)
Telly Savalas (Ernst Stavro Blofeld)
Gabriele Ferzetti (Marc Ange Draco)
Ilse Steppat (Irma Bunt)
Yuri Borienko (Grunther)
Bernard Lee (M)
Lois Maxwell (Miss Moneypenny)
Desmond Llewelyn (Q)
George Baker (Sir Hilary Bray)
Angela Scoular (Ruby Bartlett)
Bernard Horsfall (Campbell)

Joanna Lumley as one of Blofeld's "Angels of Death".

Piz Gloria – the spectacular Swiss mountain location for Blofeld's sanitarium.

George Lazenby as 007.

Bond (Sean Connery) tangles with diamond smuggler Peter Franks (Joe Robinson).

Amsterdam – where Bond first encounters Tiffany Case.

Harlem, New York City — mean streets for 007.

DIAMONDS ARE FOREVER (1971)

Cast
Sean Connery (James Bond)
Jill St John (Tiffany Case)
Charles Gray (Ernst Stavro Blofeld)
Jimmy Dean (Willard Whyte)
Putter Smith (Mr Kidd)
Bruce Glover (Mr Wint)
Joseph Furst (Dr Metz)
Bruce Cabot (Bert Saxby)
Norman Burton (Felix Leiter)
Bernard Lee (M)
Lois Maxwell (Miss Moneypenny)
Desmond Llewelyn (Q)
Lana Wood (Plenty O'Toole)
Trina Parks (Thumper)
Lola Larson (Bambi)

Producers
Harry Saltzman, Albert R. Broccoli
Director
Guy Hamilton
Screenplay
Richard Maibaum, Tom Mankiewicz
Director of Photography
Ted Moore
Production Designer
Ken Adam
Editors
Bert Bates, John W. Holmes
Music
John Barry
Title Song
Lyrics by Don Black,
sung by Shirley Bassey

Lana Wood as Plenty O'Toole – "Named after your father, perhaps?" inquired Bond.

The Nevada desert – where Willard Whyte has his hi-tech research facility.

LIVE AND LET DIE (1973)

Producers
Harry Saltzman, Albert R. Broccoli
Director
Guy Hamilton
Screenplay
Tom Mankiewicz
Director of Photography
Ted Moore
Supervising Art Director
Syd Cain
Editors
Bert Bates, Raymond Poulton,
John Shirley
Music
George Martin
Title Song
Paul and Linda McCartney, sung by
Paul McCartney and Wings

Cast
Roger Moore (James Bond)
Yaphet Kotto (Dr Kananga/Mr Big)
Jane Seymour (Solitaire)
Geoffrey Holder (Baron Samedi)
Julius W. Harris (Tee Hee)
Gloria Hendry (Rosie Carver)
Earl Jolly Brown (Whisper)
David Hedison (Felix Leiter)
Clifton James (Sheriff J. W. Pepper)
Roy Stewart (Quarrel Jr)
Bernard Lee (M)
Lois Maxwell (Miss Moneypenny)
Madeline Smith (Miss Caruso)

Clifton James as blustering, blundering Sheriff J. W. Pepper.

The Louisiana bayou – where Bond has a speedboat chase with the local police department.

Carmen de Sautoy as Saida the belly dancer – Bond's first contact during his pursuit of Scaramanga.

Saida holds a Beirut nightclub audience spellbound.

The Sardinian coast – dangerously close to Stromberg's lair.

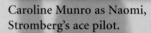

Caroline Munro as Naomi, Stromberg's ace pilot.

THE MAN WITH THE GOLDEN GUN
(1974)

Producers
Harry Saltzman, Albert R. Broccoli
Director
Guy Hamilton
Screenplay
Richard Maibaum, Tom Mankiewicz
Directors of Photography
Ted Moore, Oswald Morris
Production Designer
Peter Murton
Editors
John Shirley, Raymond Poulton
Music
John Barry
Title Song
Lyrics by Don Black, sung by Lulu

Cast
Roger Moore (James Bond)
Christopher Lee (Francisco Scaramanga)
Britt Ekland (Mary Goodnight)
Maud Adams (Andrea Anders)
Hervé Villechaize (Nick Nack)
Richard Loo (Hai Fat)
Chan Yiu Lam (Chula)
Soon-Taik Oh (Lieutenant Hip)
Clifton James (Sheriff J. W. Pepper)
Bernard Lee (M)
Lois Maxwell (Miss Moneypenny)
Desmond Llewelyn (Q)

Hervé Villechaize as Scaramanga's henchman Nick Nack.

THE SPY WHO LOVED ME (1977)

Producer
Albert R. Broccoli
Director
Lewis Gilbert
Screenplay
Christopher Wood, Richard Maibaum
Director of Photography
Claude Renoir
Production Designer
Ken Adam
Editor
John Glen
Music
Marvin Hamlisch
Title Song
"Nobody Does It Better", lyrics by Carole Bayer Sager, sung by Carly Simon

Cast
Roger Moore (James Bond)
Barbara Bach (Major Anya Amasova)
Curt Jurgens (Karl Stromberg)
Richard Kiel (Jaws)
Milton Reid (Sandor)
Caroline Munro (Naomi)
Walter Gotell (General Gogol)
Bernard Lee (M)
Lois Maxwell (Miss Moneypenny)
Desmond Llewelyn (Q)
Geoffrey Keen (Frederick Gray)
Shane Rimmer (Captain Carter)

Roger Moore as 007 stays cool under pressure with Barbara Bach as Anya, the spy who loves him.

The island of Phuket – Scaramanga's hideaway.

The Great Pyramid at Giza, Egypt – where Bond's contact Fekkesh succumbs to Jaws' bite.

MOONRAKER (1979)

Producer
Albert R. Broccoli
Executive Producer
Michael G. Wilson
Director
Lewis Gilbert
Screenplay
Christopher Wood
Director of Photography
Jean Tournier
Production Designer
Ken Adam
Editor
John Glen
Music
John Barry
Title Song
Lyrics by Hal David,
sung by Shirley Bassey

Cast
Roger Moore (James Bond)
Lois Chiles (Holly Goodhead)
Michael Lonsdale (Hugo Drax)
Richard Kiel (Jaws)
Corinne Clery (Corinne Dufour)
Toshiro Suga (Chang)
Bernard Lee (M)
Lois Maxwell (Miss Moneypenny)
Desmond Llewelyn (Q)
Emily Bolton (Manuela)
Geoffrey Keen (Frederick Gray)
Blanche Ravelec (Dolly)
Walter Gotell (General Gogol)

Geoffrey Keen as British government minister Frederick Gray.

St Mark's Place, Venice – where Bond scatters tourists in his gondola hovercraft.

Emily Bolton as Manuela, 007's ally in Rio de Janeiro.

The Iguaçu Falls between Brazil and Argentina – down which Jaws takes a plunge.

The Italian Alps near Cortina d'Ampezzo – where Bond escapes death on the ski slopes.

John Mareno as the luckless Italian agent Ferrara, killed by Kriegler of the KGB.

FOR YOUR EYES ONLY (1981)

Producer
Albert R. Broccoli
Executive Producer
Michael G. Wilson
Director
John Glen
Screenplay
Richard Maibaum, Michael G. Wilson
Director of Photography
Alan Hume
Production Designer
Peter Lamont
Editor
John Grover
Music
Bill Conti
Title Song
Lyrics by Michael Leeson, sung by Sheena Easton

Cast
Roger Moore (James Bond)
Carole Bouquet (Melina Havelock)
Topol (Columbo)
Julian Glover (Aris Kristatos)
Michael Gothard (Emile Locque)
Cassandra Harris (Countess Lisl)
Jill Bennett (Jacoba Brink)
Lynn-Holly Johnson (Bibi)
Stephan Kalipha (Hector Gonzales)
John Wyman (Kriegler)
Bernard Lee (M)
Lois Maxwell (Miss Moneypenny)
Desmond Llewelyn (Q)
Geoffrey Keen (Frederick Gray)
James Villiers (Tanner)
Walter Gotell (General Gogol)

Desmond Llewelyn as Q, disguised as a Greek Orthodox priest. "Bless me father for I have sinned," says Bond. "That's putting it mildly, 007," remarks Q.

Corfu – where Kristatos has his lair.

163

OCTOPUSSY
(1983)

Producer
Albert R. Broccoli
Executive Producer
Michael G. Wilson
Director
John Glen
Scriptwriters
George MacDonald Fraser, Richard
Maibaum, Michael G. Wilson
Director of Photography
Alan Hume
Production Designer
Peter Lamont
Supervising Editor
John Grover
Music
John Barry
Title Song
"All Time High", lyrics by
Tim Rice, sung by Rita Coolidge

Cast
Roger Moore (James Bond)
Maud Adams (Octopussy)
Louis Jourdan (Kamal Khan)
Kabir Bedi (Gobinda)
Steven Berkoff (General Orlov)
Vijay Amritraj (Vijay)
Kristina Wayborn (Magda)
Robert Brown (M)
Lois Maxwell (Miss Moneypenny)
Desmond Llewelyn (Q)
Geoffrey Keen (Frederick Gray)
Douglas Wilmer (Jim Fanning)
Albert Moses (Sadruddin)
Walter Gotell (General Gogol)
David and Tony Meyer
(Mischka & Grischka)
Tina Hudson (Bianca)
Michaela Clavell
(Penelope Smallbone)

Michaela Clavell as Miss
Moneypenny's assistant,
Penelope Smallbone.

Paris' Eiffel Tower - up which Bond
pursues the murderous May Day.

Robert Brown as M, dressed
for the Ascot races.

A VIEW TO A KILL
(1985)

Producers
Albert R. Broccoli, Michael G. Wilson
Director
John Glen
Screenplay
Richard Maibaum, Michael G. Wilson
Director of Photography
Alan Hume
Production Designer
Peter Lamont
Editor
Peter Davies
Music
John Barry
Title Song
Lyrics and performed
by Duran Duran

Cast
Roger Moore (James Bond)
Christopher Walken (Max Zorin)
Grace Jones (May Day)
Tanya Roberts (Stacey Sutton)
Patrick Macnee (Sir Godfrey Tibbett)
Willoughby Gray (Dr Carl Mortner)
Partick Bauchau (Scarpine)
Fiona Fullerton (Pola Ivanova)
Daniel Benzali (W. G. Howe)
Manning Redwood (Bob Conley)
David Yip (Chuck Lee)
Robert Brown (M)
Lois Maxwell (Miss Moneypenny)
Desmond Llewelyn (Q)
Geoffrey Keen (Frederick Gray)
Walter Gotell (General Gogol)

Udaipur, India – where
villainous Kamal Khan
has his palace.

Alison Doody as May Day's
ice-cool assistant, Jenny Flex.

One of Octopussy's
wayward girls.

San Francisco's Golden Gate Bridge – scene of Zorin's fall.

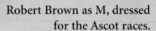

The Tangier rooftops – over which Bond escapes after shooting General Pushkin.

Virginia Hey as Rubavitch, Pushkin's girlfriend.

LICENCE TO KILL
(1989)

Producers
Albert R. Broccoli,
Michael G. Wilson
Director
John Glen
Screenplay
Richard Maibaum
Michael G. Wilson
Director of Photography
Alec Mills
Production Designer
Peter Lamont
Editor
John Grover
Music
Michael Kamen
Title Song
Lyrics by Narada Michael Walden,
Jeffrey Cohen, Walter Afanasieff,
sung by Gladys Knight

Cast
Timothy Dalton (James Bond)
Carey Lowell (Pam Bouvier)
Talisa Soto (Lupe Lamora)
Robert Davi (Franz Sanchez)
Anthony Zerbe (Milton Krest)
Everett McGill (Killifer)
Wayne Newton (Joe Butcher)
Benicio Del Toro (Dario)
Anthony Starke (Truman-Lodge)
Don Stroud (Heller)
David Hedison (Felix Leiter)
Priscilla Barnes (Della Leiter)
Frank McRae (Sharkey)
Robert Brown (M)
Caroline Bliss (Miss Moneypenny)
Desmond Llewelyn (Q)
Cary-Hiroyuki Tagawa (Kwang)

Caroline Bliss as Miss Moneypenny, whose invitation – "Any time you want to stop by and listen to my Barry Manilow collection …" – Bond politely declines.

THE LIVING DAYLIGHTS (1987)

Producers
Albert R. Broccoli, Michael G. Wilson
Director
John Glen
Screenplay
Richard Maibaum, Michael G. Wilson
Director of Photography
Alec Mills
Production Designer
Peter Lamont
Editor
John Grover, Peter Davies
Music
John Barry
Title Song
performed by a ha

Cast
Timothy Dalton (James Bond)
Maryam d'Abo (Kara Milovy)
Jeroen Krabbe (General Georgi Koskov)
Joe Don Baker (Brad Whitaker)
Andreas Wisniewski (Necros)
John Rhys-Davies
(General Leonid Pushkin)
Art Malik (Kamran Shah)
Thomas Wheatley (Saunders)
Robert Brown (M)
Caroline Bliss (Miss Moneypenny)
Desmond Llewelyn (Q)
Geoffrey Keen (Frederick Gray)
John Terry (Felix Leiter)
Walter Gotell (General Gogol)

Art Malik as mujaheddin guerrilla leader Kamran Shah.

Florida's Key West – where Bond and Pam Bouvier battle a drug gang.

The desert town of Quarzazate, Morocco – the location for the mujaheddin HQ.

Timothy Dalton as 007.

The Cuban jungle – where Janus has its HQ.

Joe Don Baker as Jack Wade, 007's CIA contact in St Petersburg.

TOMORROW NEVER DIES (1997)

Producers
Michael G. Wilson, Barbara Broccoli
Director
Roger Spottiswoode
Screenplay
Bruce Feirstein
Director of Photography
Robert Elswit
Production Designer
Allan Cameron
Editors
Dominique Fortin, Michel Arcand
Music
David Arnold
Title Song
Lyrics by Sheryl Crow
and Mitchell Froom,
sung by Sheryl Crow

Cast
Pierce Brosnan (James Bond)
Michelle Yeoh (Wai Lin)
Jonathan Pryce (Elliot Carver)
Teri Hatcher (Paris Carver)
Gotz Otto (Stamper)
Ricky Jay (Henry Gupta)
Vincent Schiavelli (Dr Kaufman)
Joe Don Baker (Jack Wade)
Judi Dench (M)
Desmond Llewelyn (Q)
Samantha Bond (Miss Moneypenny)
Geoffrey Palmer (Admiral Roebuck)
Colin Salmon (Robinson)
Cecilia Thomsen (Prof. Bergstrom)

Cecilia Thomsen as Professor of Linguistics Inga Bergstrom.

GOLDENEYE (1995)

Presented by
Albert R. Broccoli
Producers
Michael G. Wilson, Barbara Broccoli
Director
Martin Campbell
Screenplay
Jeffrey Caine, Bruce Feirstein
Story
Michael France
Director of Photography
Phil Meheux
Production Designer
Peter Lamont
Editor
Terry Rawlings
Music
Eric Serra
Title Song
Title song by Bono and The Edge,
sung by Tina Turner

Cast
Pierce Brosnan (James Bond)
Izabella Scorupco (Natalya Simonova)
Sean Bean (Alec Trevelyan)
Famke Janssen (Xenia Onatopp)
Gottfried John (General Ourumov)
Alan Cumming (Boris Grishenko)
Joe Don Baker (Jack Wade)
Robbie Coltrane (Valentin Zukovsky)
Judi Dench (M)
Desmond Llewelyn (Q)
Samantha Bond (Miss Moneypenny)
Michael Kitchen (Bill Tanner)
Tcheky Karyo (Dimitri Mishkin)

Tcheky Karyo as Dimitri Mishkin, the Russian defence minister.

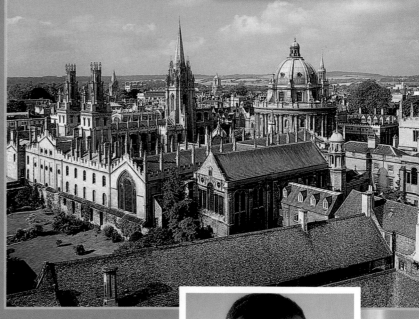

Oxford – where 007 learns a whole new language!

St Petersburg – where Bond pursues Natalya's kidnappers' car in a T55 tank.

Colin Salmon as Robinson of MI6.

Patrick Malahide as a
shifty banker, Lachaise.

Bilbao, Spain – where Bond takes the money and runs.

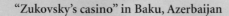

Maria Grazia Cuccinotta as the
explosive Cigar Girl.

THE WORLD IS NOT ENOUGH (1999)

Producers
Michael G. Wilson, Barbara Broccoli
Director
Michael Apted
Screenplay
Neal Purvis & Robert Wade
and Bruce Feirstein
Director of Photography
Adrian Biddle
Production Designer
Peter Lamont
Editor
Jim Clark
Music
David Arnold
Title Song
Written and performed
by Garbage

Cast
Pierce Brosnan (James Bond)
Robert Carlyle (Renard)
Sophie Marceau (Elektra King)
Denise Richards (Dr Christmas Jones)
Robbie Coltrane (Valentin Zukovsky)
Judi Dench (M)
David Calder (Sir Robert King)
Desmond Llewelyn (Q)
John Cleese (Q's assistant)
Samantha Bond (Miss Moneypenny)
Michael Kitchen (Bill Tanner)
Colin Salmon (Robinson)
John Seru (Gabor)
Claude-Oliver Rudolph (Col. Akakievich)
Ulrich Thomsen (Sacha Davidov)
Goldie (The Bull)
Maria Grazia Cuccinotta (The Cigar Girl)
Serena Scott Thomas (Dr Molly
Warmflash)
Patrick Malahide (Lachaise)

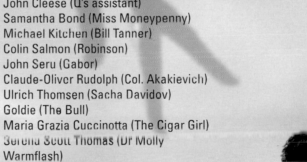

Goldie as The Bull
Valentin Zukovsky's
treacherous henchman.

A casino hostess
welcomes Bond.

"Zukovsky's casino" in Baku, Azerbaijan

Explosive action scenes set in the Demilitarized Zone between North and South Korea were filmed at the Army Driving Training Area at Aldershot in England.

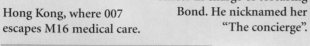

Tymarah as the North Korean officer in charge of torturing Bond. He nicknamed her "The concierge".

Hong Kong, where 007 escapes M16 medical care.

The Thames Embankment near MI6 headquarters.

DIE ANOTHER DAY

(2002)

Producers
Michael G. Wilson, Barbara Broccoli
Director
Lee Tamahori
Screenplay
Neal Purvis & Robert Wade
Director of Photography
David Tattersall
Editor
Andrew MacRitchie, Christian Wagner
Music
David Arnold
Title Song
Written by Mirwais Ahmadzaï and Madonna;
performed by Madonna

Cast
Pierce Brosnan (James Bond)
Halle Berry (Jinx)
Toby Stephens (Gustav Graves)
Rosamund Pike (Miranda Frost)
Rick Yune (Zao)
Judi Dench (M)
John Cleese (Q)
Michael Madsen   (Damian Falco)
Will Yun Lee (Colonel Moon)
Kenneth Tsang (General Moon)
Emilio Echevarría (Raoul)
Mikhail Gorevoy (Vlad)
Lawrence Makoare (Mr. Kil)
Colin Salmon (Charles Robinson)
Samantha Bond (Miss Moneypenny)
Ben Wee (Desk Clerk)
Ho Yi (Mr Chang)
Rachel Grant (Peaceful Fountains of Desire)
Simón Andreu (Dr Alvarez)
Mark Dymond (Mr Van Bierk)

Colin Salmon as MI6's Robinson, Bond's friend.

Emilio Echevarría as Raoul, a "sleeper agent" who helps Bond find Zao in Havana, Cuba.

John Cleese as Q, MI6's overseer of "the ultimate in British engineering."

Daniel Craig makes his debut as James Bond.

A building site in Madagascar – where Bond goes hunting a terrorist freerunning bomber.

CASINO ROYALE

(2006)

Producers
Michael G. Wilson, Barbara Broccoli
Director
Martin Campbell
Screenplay
Neal Purvis, Robert Wade, Paul Haggis
Director of Photography
Phil Meheux
Music
David Arnold

Cast
Daniel Craig (James Bond)
Dame Judi Dench (M)
Eva Green (Vesper Lynd)
Mads Mikkelsen (Le Chiffre)
Jeffrey Wright (Felix Leiter)
Giancarlo Giannini (Mathis)
Caterina Murino (Solange)
Simon Abkarian (Dimitrios)
Tobias Menzies (Villiers)
Ivana Milicevic (Valenka)
Clemens Schick (Kratt)
Ludger Pistor (Mendel)
Claudio Santamaria (Carlos)
Sebastien Foucan (Mollaka)

Nassau, Bahamas – a paradise where Bond encounters the evil Le Chiffre.

Montenegro – home of the famous Casino Royale.

Eva Green plays Vesper Lynd

The Grand Canal, Venice – the perfect setting for a romance, or a tragedy.

Marc Forster, *Quantum of Solace*'s director.

Olga Kurylenko as Camille.

Bond (Daniel Craig) incurs the wrath of M (Judi Dench).

QUANTUM OF SOLACE
(2008)

Producers
Michael G. Wilson and Barbara Broccoli
Director
Marc Forster
Screenplay
Neil Purvis & Robert Wade, Paul Haggis
Executive Producers
Anthony Waye, Callum McDougall
Music by
David Arnold
Production Designer
Dennis Gassner
Director of Photography
Roberto Schaefer A.S.C.
Editors
Matt Chesse, Richard Pearson

Cast
Daniel Craig (James Bond)
Olga Kurylenko (Camille)
Mathieu Amalric (Dominic Greene)
Judi Dench (M)
Jeffrey Wright (Felix Leiter)
Giancarlo Giannini (René Mathis)
Gemma Arterton (Agent Fields)
Anatole Taubman (Elvis)
Jesper Christiansen (Mr White)
David Harbour (Gregg Beam)
Neil Jackson (Mr Slate)
Tim Pigott-Smith (Foreign Secretary)
Joaquín Cosio (General Medrano)

Bond's dust-covered Aston Martin enters the picturesque, medieval centre of Siena, Italy.

Mathieu Amalric as ruthless business mogul Dominic Greene.

A marble quarry near Siena – scene of a breakneck car chase.

On location in the Atacama desert, northern Chile.

Joaquín Cosio as the brutal General Medrano.

Gemma Arterton as Agent Fields of MI6.

Bregenz, Austria, where Bond tangles with Greene and his crew.

Anatole Taubman as Greene's sidekick Elvis.

Tim Pigott-Smith as the British Foreign Secretary.

INDEX

INDEX

ACKNOWLEDGMENTS

Picture Credits

The publisher would like to thank the following for their kind permission to reproduce their photographs:

a=above; c=centre; b=below; l=left; r=right; t=top

Axiom: Chris Caldicott 152tc.
The J. Allan Cash Photolibrary: 148tr, 149crb.
Corbis UK Ltd: Bettmann 17tr; Catherine Karnow 149tr.
Robert Harding Picture Library:
40tl, 146br, 147br, 149clb, 150tc, 150cl, 151tl, 151bl; 152cr; C. Bowman 152bl.
Hutchison Library: 147tc, 147tr, 149cl; J Henderson 144bl.
Image Bank: 17tc, 146cr.
Impact Photos: Mark Henley 144bl.
Magnum: Dennis Stock 144br.
N.H.P.A.: 145tr.
Science Photo Library: 49br.
Spectrum Colour Library:
80cl, 145cl, 146tl, 147bl, 151cr.
The Stock Market: 150br; Kunio Owaki 54c.
Art Directors & TRIP: A. Tovy 107br; Tibor Bognar 148bl.
Digital film at the *Moving Picture Company:*
118tl, 119bl, 124tr, 125tm, 125br.
Alamy Images: FAN travelstock 154br.
Corbis: Robert Matheson 154tr.
Photolibrary: Japack Photo Library 154cl.
Alamy Images: Steve Allen Travel Photography 155cr.
Getty Images: Mark Harwood 155 br; Don Klumpp 155cl.

All other images © Dorling Kindersley
For further information see: www.dkimages.com

Dorling Kindersley and the writer would like to thank the following for their help in producing this book:

Jenni McMurrie, Keith Snelgrove, John Parkinson, Meg Simmonds and Tim Ryan at Eon Productions, Piccadilly; Doug Redenius of the Ian Fleming Foundation, Illinois; Wing Commander Ken Wallis for help on the "Little Nellie" pages; Mark Bullimore for advice on the Q Boat, the Avalanche Suit and much more; Roger Stowers at Aston Martin, Newport Pagnell; Peter Nelson and Cars of the Stars Museum, Keswick; Cliff Plackett at Egerton's Transport, Thornthwaite; Malcolm Bord of Gold Coin Exchange, London; Michael Shorrocks of MBI Inc.; Lt Commander Martin Cropper; J. W. "Corkey" Fornof for help on the Acrostar pages; Nicola Kingman of The Moving Picture Company, London; Lynn Bresler for the Index; Elizabeth Bacon for research assistance; Dan Newman and Keith Newell for design assistance.

Special photography by Jerry Young:
Little Nellie case, Aston Martin DB5, jacket; Aston Martin DB5, half title page; Little Nellie, title page; "The Bond Look", pp 10-13; "Box of Tricks", pp 32-33; "The Bondmobile", pp 36-37; "Little Nellie", pp 46-47; "Wet Nellie", pp 68-69; "The Acrostar", pp 82-83; "Aston Martin V8", pp 94-95; "Remote Control", pp 112-113; "The Q Boat", 120-121; "Escape Pod", p 123; "The BMW Z8", pp 124-125; "Torture Chair", pp 126.